Money Lessons for Kids with Mia & Milo

Financial Literacy Made Fun in an Adventurous Story of Budgeting, Saving, & Investing

Raman Keane

Illustrations & Cover Design by

Diogo Alves

Table of Contents

Chapter 1

Goldie and Chip

Milo and Mia are energetic eight-year-olds who love doing things together. They are not just siblings but best friends and have been inseparable since birth.

Though Milo and Mia are twins, they differ, as the moon differs from the sun.

Milo is curious and the jokester of the two, always ready to explore new things. He is more cautious than his sister, but he has a strong sense of curiosity and loves solving puzzles. He is the type of boy who likes asking questions and knowing what is happening next.

He enjoys reading about knights and explorers and dreams of finding hidden treasures on the beach someday. When they go to the park with their mother, you will always find Milo on the monkey bars swinging about.

Milo's physical appearance, with golden blond hair and striking blue eyes, is in contrast to his sister's. With Mia's chocolate brown hair and hazel eyes that miss nothing, they are quite the sight when they go on adventures.

Mia is imaginative and loves to dream up stories. Whenever she is playing with Milo, she is always the one who comes up with the narrative of their adventures. Mia wants to be a writer one day and looks forward to other people reading and enjoying her imagination.

Mia is on the bolder side compared to her brother. She takes risks without thinking them through and enjoys every moment of it. If there is something to jump off, she will do it without any hesitation.

She tells everyone she meets for the first time that she is the oldest, even if it is just by one minute.

The twins share a room, and although it can get crazy at times, they enjoy being able to go on adventures with each other whenever they want to. Mia's love for animals rivals Milo's love for adventures. Her side of their room is filled with stuffed animals and her drawings of all her favorite ones. Milo has posters of adventurers and pirates everywhere; he even made some of them himself.

Out of everything the twins do, they love playing in their grandparent's attic the most. There is just something about the dusty place that makes it feel like a time machine. They have spent many of their days in the warm attic, reenacting epic battles with dragons and dangerous adventures to frozen lands.

A day does not pass without them asking their mother to visit their grandparents.

Luckily for Mia and Milo, they stay right next door to their grandparents and go over to their grandparents for some playtime at every opportunity they get. They still have to convince their grandma to let them play in the attic, but she has not put up much of a fight lately.

The day started like any other day for the twins.

They got up and ready for school, where they learned about numbers and played outside. After school, they got home and ate a snack before they pleaded with their mother to let them go next door and visit their grandparents.

"Please, Mom," Mia gives her mother puppy dog eyes. Their mother sighs and smiles at them.

"Okay, we can go visit, but you first need to finish your math homework." The twins waste no time as they run over to the living room table and start with their homework. Working together, they finish everything within record time.

They enter their grandparents' house with a joyful shout. They ran over to their grandmother and greeted her with hugs and kisses.

"Gran," Milo looks up at his grandmother as she is still hugging him. "Can we please go and play in the attic?" he asks her while batting his eyelashes.

Their grandmother laughs at them and nods her head yes. The twins cheer in glee and run up to the attic.

"What game do you want to play today, Milo?" Mia asks as they walk into the attic.

"Let's play pirates and try to find hidden treasure in the attic!" Milo suggested with an excited smile. Mia agrees, and the two start exploring the attic, looking for new treasures.

They face many foes and avoid booby traps on their hunt for treasure.

"Look, Mia!" Milo calls out to his sister as he stands on top of an old couch they are using for their ship. "I found another island that might be filled with treasure!" He points to a random stack of boxes in the corner of the attic that can only be seen when you stand on something high.

Together, they move to the stack of boxes, pretending to fight invisible enemies on their way there. Out of breath from their battle, they stand in front of a box and admire it, wondering what they might find inside.

"Wow," Whispers Mia. "This is the most beautiful treasure chest I have ever seen." Her eyes fill with excitement as she looks over at her brother. Milo gives her a lopsided smile, just as excited as she is to find something they have never found before.

"I care more about the loot inside the chest." He says as he dramatically opens the box. What they found inside the old box was not what they expected at all. Nestled between old coats and some books was a real chest! One that looked like all Milo's drawings of a treasure chest.

"No way!" Milo exclaims with glee. Wasting no time, he slowly pulls it out of the box and puts it on the ground between them.

Together, they open the chest and are surprised by what they find.

Inside the chest, they find a dusty, ancient-looking map and a golden compass. Milo looks up at Mia.

"Do you think this is a real treasure map?" he whispers to his sister with wide eyes.

"I don't know." Mia shrugs her shoulder and reaches for the map.

As Mia is reaching for the map, so does Milo. The twins touch the map at the same time, and it comes to life, revealing a shimmering golden path on it. Milo and Mia stumble back as the map flies out of the box and into the air.

In amazement, they look on as the map grows arms and legs, smiling brightly at them. They hear a rattle in the box, and the compass jumps out and joins the map. Milo and Mia look at each other with big eyes, not sure if what they are seeing is real.

"Hello! My name is Goldie, the map." The map introduces herself in a cheerful voice, ignoring the twin's confused looks. "And this is my best friend, Chip the Compass."

Chip winks at them as Goldie introduces him. Milo and Mia giggle at this, sharing a gap-toothed smile. Their confusion and uncertainty quickly replaced with excitement.

"How long have you been in the chest?" Milo asks. He wonders why they had never explored this corner of the attic before.

"Oh, it's hard to say." Goldie looks around the room a bit before she answers them. "Time works differently where we come from. We have been guides of many curious minds over the years."

"We've been here since the beginning of time," Chip interrupts Goldie, sticking out his tongue at her when she gives him the stink eye.

"As I was saying, we have guided many curious minds over the years." Goldie continues after clearing her throat.

"Do you want to go on an adventure with us?" she smiles even brighter at them and wiggles her eyebrows in anticipation.

"What type of adventure?" Mia asks Goldie curiously.

"A magical adventure filled with many new friends and puzzles!" Chip answers for Goldie, dancing around the twins to music only he can hear.

"A journey to learn more about money," Goldie clarifies what Chip had said.

"Money?" Mia asks, a bit uncertain. What is there to learn about money?

"Yes! There are many things you still don't know about money." Goldie informs the twins.

Mia starts nodding her head, happy with the answers they received. She is excited to start with the adventure right now.

Milo turns to Mia and takes her hand in his, pulling her away from Goldie and Chip.

"I don't know if this is a good idea, Mia," Milo whispers to his sister as they look back at Goldie and Chip, who are now chatting with each other and waiting for them patiently.

"Why?" asks Mia. "We get to go on a real magical adventure. Aren't you excited?" she asks her brother, not bothering with whispering.

"I am excited," Milo says a little defensively. "I just think we need to go ask Mom and Dad first." Milo plays with his fingers, something he only does when he is nervous.

"What if they come looking for us, and we aren't here?" Mia considers her brother's words before nodding her head, agreeing with the idea of asking their parents first.

"Goldie," Mia calls out to the glowing map. "We really want to go on the adventure with you and Chip."

"Excellent!" Goldie chirps.

"But first, we need to go ask our parents if we can go with you," Mia tells Goldie, standing in front of her.

Goldie nods in understanding.

Milo and Mia run out of the attic and downstairs to the kitchen, where their parents are having some coffee.

"Mom, Dad!" Milo calls out as they run into the kitchen.

"Can we please go on a magical adventure with Goldie and Chip?" Mia interrupts, jumping from one foot to the other. Their parents look at each other before they turn their attention back to the twins.

"Where are Goldie and Chip?" their mother asks as she places their empty mug in the kitchen sink.

"In the attic," answers Milo as he points in the direction of the stairs.

"Lead the way, kiddos," comes the instruction from their dad. Without wasting another second, Milo and Mia start speed walking up the stairs, trying to get their parents to go faster.

"Come on, Mom! You're so slow," complains Mia as she pulls on her mother's arm.

"I'm coming, I'm coming," her mother laughs at her. Once in the attic, Mia calls out to Goldie and Chip.

Goldie and Chip appear out of nowhere and greet the twins' parents.

"Hello, Sasha," Milo's eyes jump from his mom to his new friends.

"You know my mom?" he asks Goldie.

"Yes, we went on many adventures with your mother when she was your age. She was one of my favorites,"

Goldie says with a wink. The twins stare at their parents in shock.

"What adventure will you be taking them on?" the twins' dad asks Goldie.

Chip zooms around his head a few times before he stops and answers the question.

"We're going to teach them about money!" Chip sings.

Milo and Mia's mother gives them a stern look. "You can go on your adventure, but you need to be back in time for dinner, okay?"

They nod their heads, no longer able to contain their excitement. The twins wave goodbye to their parents and turn to Goldie and Chip.

A pink and blue light fills the room, and a magical portal opens up in front of them.

"Let's go adventuring!" Goldie calls out, and all four of them walk through the magical portal that Goldie created.

Learning with Milo and Mia.

Answer the questions below to see if you can remember what Goldie and Chip taught us in this chapter. Choose one correct answer below.

What adventure will Milo and Mia be going on?

A. An adventure to learn about money.

B. They are going to the zoo.

C. They are going on an outer space adventure.

Do you think kids need to know how to work with money?

A. Yes

B. No

Would you go on a fun adventure if a stranger asked you?

A. Yes! Learning is fun.

B. Maybe let me ask my parents first.

C. No, magic and adventures sound boring to me.

Ask yourself these questions and think about your answers.

1. If you found a magical map and compass, what kind of adventures would you want to go on?

2. Why do you think it is important to learn about money, even for kids?

Chapter 2

The Land of Money

With a whoosh and a bang, Milo and Mia find themselves standing in what looks like a town center. All around them are stacks of paper money and piles of coins. They turn in a circle as they try to take everything in at once.

"Wow," Milo whispers under his breath. "How did we get here?" he asks Goldie with wide eyes.

"We traveled by portal." She answers him, giving the impression that he is supposed to know this already.

"Can you create a portal that can go anywhere?" Mia asks Goldie, her attention on the piles of coins closest to them.

"I can only make portals to places I have been with my friends before," comes the answer from Goldie. "

Milo is no longer paying attention to the conversation between his sister and Goldie. He has come across something he has never seen before. He walks closer to a digital screen on a wall close to them, and Chip follows him.

"Chip, what is that?" he asks as his eyes run over the screen. It is filled with numbers and symbols he has never seen before.

"That is a digital screen showing cryptocurrency," Chip answers. Milo frowns at Chip. He has no idea what cryptocurrency is. Chip sees the question in his eyes and smiles mysteriously.

"You will find out what it is a bit later," he answers the question in Milo's eyes.

Milo turns back to the screen and looks at it in fascination, excited to learn more about whatever cryptocurrency is. He has never seen anything like it before. He's not sure he even knows how to explain to someone what he is looking at. As Milo admires the digital screens, Mia creeps closer to a pile of coins next to them.

"Can I Take some of these coins," Mia asks Goldie as she stretches her hand out to take a coin on top of the pile. Goldie comes to float between her and the pile of coins, a stern expression on her face.

"No can-do, little missy," she answered her whispered question. "These coins are not for us to take. They belong to King Coin." Goldie informs her. Mia pulls her hand back and looks up at Goldie with a slight pout on her face. She really wants a gold coin to take home and show her mom.

"Why don't we go say hello to the King?" Goldie suggests after seeing the disappointment in Mia's eyes. Milo and Mia agree, and together, the four adventurers walk down the streets.

It does not take them long at all to reach the big castle where King Coin stays. Goldie and Chip greet the guards like old friends and request to see King Coin.

"Hello, Pau. It is lovely to see you."

They follow one of the guards down the long hallway and into the throne room. Mia lets out a gasp. The throne room is filled with piles of paper money and coins. Some stacks are so big that they even touch the roof.

"Hello, little ones. Welcome to the Land of Money." The friendly king greets the twins.

King Coin is sitting on a throne made out of the biggest gold coins Mia has ever seen. He is wearing a robe decorated with the shiniest coins that reflect the light of the chandelier, and in his hand, he is holding a beautiful scepter with a big coin on top.

"Goldie told me that you guys want to learn more about money?" he says in his wise voice as he observes the twins.

"Yes, sir," Milo answers, straightening his back so that he can stand taller to show respect to the king.

"That's good, that's good." The king says while making a humming sound. He stands up from his throne and walks down to them.

"Join me for a walk around the land. There are so many things I want to show you." King Coin says, excited to have someone new to show the Land of Money to. He leads them out of the throne room and into the castle gardens. The walk is brisk and filled with beautiful scenes. They make their way into town, down busy streets filled with people.

They come to a stop at the edge of a market. There are people walking around with baskets filled with a variety of different things. The people go around and talk to each other, sometimes in groups of two or three. After a few minutes of talking, they would either walk away or give each other things out of their baskets. Swapping one thing for another.

"Tell me what you see, kids." Milo and Mia take in the scene in front of them, not entirely sure what King Coin wants them to see.

"It's a market," Mia speaks up first as she watches everything. "It looks like people are giving each other gifts."

"This is a market, but they aren't giving each other gifts." The king says as he lays a kind hand on Mia's head. He lets go of Mia's head and stands in front of them.

"They aren't giving each other gifts. They are trading." The wise king tells them. He looks at the twins with his kind eyes, seeing the questions swimming around in their heads.

"Trading?" Milo asks, frowning. He looks at the people walking around in the market, trying to see what King Coin means.

"They are exchanging one thing for another. Look." The king says, pointing to a farmer trading three apples for one loaf of bread. Milo and Mia observe the trade happen with hungry eyes, wanting to understand what is happening.

"Before we had paper money and bank accounts, people used trade to get what they needed. If I had apples and needed bread, I would trade the bake for some." The king explains to the twins.

"We didn't always have paper money?" Milo questions the king. Chip, next to him, nods his head and speaks up before the king has the opportunity to talk.

"Yeah! It is only in the last few hundred years that humans have been using paper money." Chip tells Milo, excited to share some history with them.

"Chip, this is King Coins' demonstration. Remember?" Goldie reminds Chip. With a giggle, Chip apologizes to the king and promises to stay quiet until the end of the tour.

The king laughs with Chip and accepts his apology. King Coin starts walking, and everyone follows him. He points to historical landmarks in the town and continues to share the history of money with Milo and Mia.

He comes to a stop in front of a display case in the center of the town. The display is filled with many unfamiliar things.

"Over time, people noticed there is a problem with trading." The King turns his attention towards the display case as he speaks to the twins.

"This case is a physical representation of how money evolved over the years." King Coin turns his back on the display and points to Milo.

"Milo, can you tell me what made people realize that trading is not effective?" the king asks Milo with a soft and caring smile. Milo looks over at the display case and thinks hard about what he saw in the market.

"Well," Milo says, a bit uncertain. "Maybe people couldn't agree on what the value of things is?" Milo states uncertainly. King Coin nods his head and encourages him to continue. This gives Milo more confidence, so he continues.

"What if I think bread is worth three apples, but the farmer thinks it is worth two?" King Coin smiles at Milo like a proud mentor. He gives Milo a high-five.

"Excellent answer, Milo. That is exactly what happened. People couldn't agree on the value of things, so they needed a common medium of trade."

"One of the first things used as a form of money was the Cowry Shells." King Coin points at beautiful shells displayed in the window. Mia steps closer and admires the shells, understanding why people wanted more of them.

"Everyone agreed that Cowry Shells could be exchanged for goods and services." King Coin nods along with Goldie's words.

"Later, precious metals like silver and gold were discovered, and quickly became a new way to trade for things." King Coin points to a gold nugget in the display case.

"Gold was really hard to get, so that made it extra valuable." Chip intercedes with a wiggle of his eyebrows.

Mia puts her hand up in the air, wanting to get King Coin's attention without being rude. The king nods his head at her, giving her permission to speak.

"We still use gold today, don't we, King Coin?"

"That is right," Mia smiles brightly at her brother at the king's confirmation, happy that she knows something about money that he doesn't know.

"As gold grew in popularity to pay for things, people couldn't carry all their gold around with them. So, the local goldsmiths started storing them and giving people receipts for the gold they kept safe." King Coin points to a piece of very old-looking paper.

"People would use these receipts to pay for things instead of gold." King Coin has the full attention of the twins as they hang on to every word he says. They are fascinated by the history of money.

"As time went on, people started using money and coins as we know them today. Everyone agreed on the value of the paper money and coins."

"Eventually, as technology improved and the world population grew, people started putting their money in banks. Using their bank cards or even phones to get their money when they need it." Continues King Coin.

The twins look at the window displaying all the different types of money over the centuries. Milo noticed a tablet in the window with the same numbers and symbols he saw when they first arrived in the Land of Currency.

"King Coin," Milo calls out to the king. "What is that used for? Goldie said it is cryptocurrency." Milo asks the king, his eyes shining with curiosity.

"Cryptocurrency is money that is only available in digital form. You can't hold it in your hands like coins or paper money." Milo's eyes widen at this. It's like having money in the computer games he plays, but it's real money.

After the king explained where the money came from, the group of friends walked around some more. Milo and Mia took in the beautiful scenery of the Land of Currency, stopping every now and then to ask the king some more questions. They make their way back to the castle and come to a stop at the gate.

"Before you move on to your next adventure, there is something you need to know." Milo and Mia turn to King Coin and give him their full attention.

"Money can be used for more than just buying nice things. It is a tool you can use to save and invest. It can help you to plan for the future and reach your dreams."

King Coin reaches into his robe pocket and pulls out two gold coins, handing one to each twin. Milo and Mia hold their gold coins in their hands in wonder, fascinated by the idea of learning how money works.

"Understanding how money works is the first step to using it wisely." The king says to them, smiling at their reaction to receiving the money.

"Thank you, King Coin. We promise to look after the coins you gave us," Mia reassures the king, putting her gold coin away in her pocket. Milo plays with the coin in his hands, not ready to put it away just yet.

"It is always wonderful spending time with you, King Coin. Thank you for the lesson on the history of money." Goldie thanks the king. King Coin nods his head in acknowledgment and says goodbye to them. They wave to him as he walks away.

"Right," Goldie says, buzzing with energy. On her, a new pathway is glowing in gold.

"Are you ready for your next adventure?" she asks the twins in a singsong voice. Milo and Mia nod their heads and start jumping up and down. Ready to move on to the next part of their adventure.

"Where are we going?" Mia asks Goldie.

"We are heading to the Piggy Palace, where we will be meeting up with Penny the Pig, Queen of the pigs."

"Whoohoo." Milo chanted, punching his fist in the air. "Come, let's go." He grabs his sister's hand and pulls her behind him as he starts running. Chip lets out a whoop of his own and joins the twins in their race to the Piggy Palace. Goldie sighs at their childlike antics.

"Wait for me," she calls out to them and zooms in their direction, determined to win the race they are all partaking in.

Learning with Milo and Mia.

Answer the questions below to see if you can remember what King Coin taught us in this chapter.

<u>What was used as one of the first forms of money ever?</u>

A. Shoelaces.
B. Cowry Shells.
C. River Rocks.

<u>Are gold and silver still valuable today?</u>

A. Yes, they are.
B. I'm not sure. Maybe?
C. No, they aren't valuable anymore.

<u>True or false: We only use paper money today.</u>

A. True.

B. False.

Ask yourself these questions and think about your answers.

1. What did you learn about the different forms of money?

2. How do you think people used to trade before money was invented?

Chapter 3

Piggy Palace

Even though Goldie had a late start to the race, she was the first one to reach the Piggy Palace. She laughs as Chip catches up to her, out of breath from the fast flying.

"Tired already," she teases him. "We just got started with our adventure." Chip sticks his tongue out at her with a smile on his face. Milo and Mia arrive at the same time and start arguing about who got there first.

"I won," Milo says with confidence, his chest pushed out in pride. Mia pushes him playfully on the shoulder.

"No, I was first." They start pushing and ticking each other as they continue to banter. It takes them a few minutes before they come to an agreement that it is a draw. Finally, after a little sibling bantering, they turn their attention to Goldie and Chip.

"Are we almost there?" Mia asks Goldie, searching around for Piggy Palace.

"Yes, we are." Goldie moves out of the way, and Mia finally notices the big pink piggy bank standing behind Goldie. She gasps and points to it.

"Look, Milo, it's a big piggy bank," Mia says excitedly. She saw one the last time she went to the shops with her mother. She really wants a piggy bank, though she is not sure what it is used for exactly. Milo turns to the direction Mia is pointing but doesn't understand her excitement.

"Why are you so excited?" he asks her with a frown. Mia sighs and rolls her eyes at her brother.

"It's cool, that's why." She states in a matter-of-fact voice. "Just look at it. Where have you ever seen a giant pink piggy bank before?" Mia raises one of her eyebrows at her brother. Milo, still clueless about why Mia is so excited, just shrugs his shoulder and turns to Goldie and Chip.

"Where is Queen of the queens?" he asks. Goldie smiles at him and points to the huge piggy bank behind them.

"She is in the Piggy Palace." Milo's eyes widen as he looks at the piggy bank in a new light. Now that he knows what to look for, he can see windows and doors leading into the piggy bank and even some piggy guards walking around and talking to each other.

"That's so cool," he comments as he waves to one piggy guard that noticed them.

"I told you," Mia said to her brother in a taunting way. Milo gives her a light shove at her retort.

They start walking towards the Piggy Palace. As they draw near to the palace, Milo notices something extra-ordinary.

"The Piggy Palace is made out of millions of small piggy banks!" He exclaims excitedly, pointing to the wall of the palace. The light of the sun is hitting the palace just right, casting a rainbow of colors to reflect the adventuring party. Milo and Mia were mesmerized by the sight.

"Beautiful, isn't it?" their attention is drawn to a re-gal-looking Pig with a shiny crown on her head. Mia gets down in a curtsy and elbows her brother to do the same. Milo bows down, a little confused.

"Lovely to see you, Queen Penny." Goldie greets the Queen as she and Chip also bow down.

"The honor is all mine," the queen answers Goldie, tipping her head in greeting. "I have been waiting for you. King Coin told me you were coming." The queen turns her attention to the twins and gives them an elegant nod of the head.

"I am Queen Penny. Queen and guardian of savings and smart money management." Mia is amazed by the queen and smiles at her brightly.

"My name is Mia, and this is my twin brother, Milo." Mia looks around the palace and admires everything as they start walking. She has never been in a place as pretty as this one before.

"What do you do as a queen?" Mia turns back to the queen and asks the question that was burning in her chest. Queen Penny laughs lightly and gestures with her hand to the room around them.

"Every piggy bank you see here represents a child like you and Milo saving the pocket money they receive." The queen answers her question.

"As Queen of saving, it is my duty to teach new minds the importance of saving and planning for the future." The twins take a closer look at all the piggy banks lining the wall. Every piggy bank is different, just like the child they belong to. Some piggy banks are covered in glitter and stickers, while other piggy banks glow a soft light.

One of the piggy banks started playing a cheerful tune, giving Mia a little fright. Queen Penny giggles and places a comforting hand on Mia's shoulder.

"There is nothing to worry about, Mia. Every time a child saves money, their piggy bank here starts playing a happy song." They continue their tour of the castle as Queen Penny points out different piggy banks as they go.

Milo notices something on one of the piggy banks they are looking at. "Queen Penny, why does this piggy bank have something written on it?"

The queen walks over to where Milo is standing and looks at the piggy bank he is talking about. On the piggy bank, written in cursive letters, is the word bicycle.

"Ah. Some kids are saving money for something they really want. Like this little boy saving his money to get a new bike." Milo looks away from the queen and back to the piggy bank.

"We can do that?" Queen Penny looks at Milo with kind eyes and nods her head.

"Yes, Milo. That is why people save their money." The queen lets her gaze roam over all the piggy banks around them. "Saving money allows us to purchase things we might not be able to afford otherwise."

"Come on, there are some wise people I want you to meet." Queen Penny leads them down a long hallway and into a big room that looks a lot like a classroom. Together, the adventurers walk to the front of the class-room and take a seat.

A group of animals walk into the room. All of them have their own sense of style. Queen Penny gestures to them as she introduces the animals.

"These are my saving champions. They will each give us tips on how to save money and work with it more re-sponsibly." The queen takes a seat next to Mia. "The floor is all yours."

The first to step forward is a piggy with a blue tie, looking a little nervous. He holds onto his tie tightly as he introduces himself.

"My name is Howard, the Habit Hero. I save some coins every day, even if it is just one." He looks over at the queen and she gives him a nod of encouragement.

"It is important to make saving money a habit. The more you save, the more you will have." Howard is growing more confident as he speaks.

"Small amounts of savings add up over time, so don't give up on it." Howard steps back in line and blushes a little when the group claps their hands for him. A hedgehog with a purple and green bow in her hair is up next.

"Hello, I'm Gloria." She introduced herself with a bright smile. "I am saving up to buy myself a new scooter. I haven't always been good at saving money. But when I set a goal and decided to save for the scooter, I became more focused and motivated." She nodded her head in a firm yes and moved back to the line.

The next champion, a tortoise with a backward cap on, takes a little longer than the rest to come forward and introduce himself. When he finally reaches the front, he starts speaking in a fast-paced way that surprises Milo and Mia.

"I am Travis. I am always on the move and keep this chalkboard with me to track my savings. Whenever I save money, I write it down. This motivates me to keep on savings, especially on the days I don't feel like it.

Thank you." Just as fast as Travis started speaking, he was done.

He slowly makes his way back to his spot in the line, and as he does so, someone else steps up. A small ferret scurries to the front and rubs his hands together nervously.

"All my friends call me the chore champ, but my real name is Chris," the ferret starts speaking in a small voice. He fidgets with his hands as he speaks. "I uh. I help my mom around the house a lot to earn extra money to save. This is helping me reach my goal faster." Chris stands there a little longer, not saying anything else.

Gloria softly calls out to him, and he scurries back in line while keeping his head low as the next champion steps forward.

"My name is Lily, and I specialize in safely saving money." A friendly ladybug introduces herself with a smile and a head nod.

"It is important to keep your money in a piggy bank or with an adult you know and trust." She says with a serious expression on her face. "It is not a nice feeling when you lose the money you worked so hard to save."

"Thank you, Lily." The queen says before gesturing to the next champion to step forward.

Next, a big bear steps forward. The bear looks a bit mean until he opens his mouth and speaks to them in a soft and calm voice.

"The name is Wesley," his deep voice rumbles. "I spend my money wisely by having daily spending goals and never spending more than I said I would." Wesley steps back into line, and he is a bear with few words.

"I am Paula!" An energetic flamingo skips forward, a big smile on her face. "And this is my identical twin sister, Franny." The flamingo steps to the side and reveals a second copy of herself.

"When our friends want to go to the toy and sweet shop, we don't always go with them." Paula looks over at her sister with a smile. They like to spend all their money in one place and try to pressure us into spending our money, too. We always say no.

"There are a lot of things we can do that are free," Franny speaks up, interrupting Paula a little.

"You don't have to spend money to have fun. You can go for a walk with your family or go play in the park with your friends," she says confidently, ruffling her feathers.

"So instead of spending money on things you don't need, you can save the money instead!" The twin flamingos thank the adventurers and the queen for listening before they fall back in line.

Queen Penny gets up from her chair and stands in front of her champions.

"Thank you so much for teaching us about responsibly saving money." She gives them a shallow curtsy, and they all bow their heads at her.

Queen Penny watches as they leave, and she waits until the last champion is out of the door before she turns her attention to the twins.

"What was your favorite part of the presentation?" she asks Milo and Mia with an excited clap of her hands.

Milo is the first to speak up. "There is so much you need to remember when saving money. My favorite champion was Travis," he says excitedly. "I want to get a book and write everything I save down. It must be so cool to see everything you have saved so far." Mia giggles at her brother's excitement.

"I liked Paula and Franny the most," Mia says after some consideration. "I think it is neat that you can save money by doing free things like walking outside."

Queen Penny was delighted by their answers. She walks over to a closet next to the door and pulls it open. She gets something out of the closet and hides it behind her back as she walks back to them.

"I enjoyed having you guys visit me. It was a delight to teach you about saving money, but sadly, our time has come to an end." Queen Penny's voice turns sad at the end of her sentence. She blinks away a few tears and removes her hand from behind her back.

With a gasp, Milo and Mia reach out, each taking a piggy bank out of Queen Penny's hand. As they hold the piggy banks in their hands, they start changing. Mia's piggy bank changes into a rainbow glitter piggy bank with her name on the side.

Milo's piggy bank turns bright blue and starts glowing. They each thank the queen and give her a big hug. Together, they put the first gold coin they received from King Coin into their piggy banks.

They feel a sense of accomplishment and excitement as they watch their piggy banks glow. They can't wait to see where their adventure takes them next.

"Thank you so much for teaching us about saving Queen Penny." Mia thanks the queen and gives her a tight hug. The twins set out with Goldie and Chip to their next destination.

Learning with Milo and Mia.

Answer the questions below to see if you can remember what Queen Penny and the saving champions taught us in this chapter. Choose one correct answer below.

How do you save your money?

A. I can save money in a piggy bank or give it to an adult to keep safe.

B. I hide it under my bed.

C. I don't save any money and spend it all.

What happens when we save little by little?

A. The money grows old, and we need to throw it away.

B. Nothing, it stays the same.

C. Your money becomes more over time as you save more.

What can you do if you don't have enough money to buy something you want?

A. Ask my parents to buy it for me.

B. I can save some of my money and buy it later.

C. try buying it even if I don't have enough money.

Ask yourself these questions and think about your answers.

1. What are some things you might want to save money for in the future?

2. How does setting goals help you save money?

Chapter 4

Gilly the Banker

Milo and Mia's magical adventure continues as Goldie teleports them to a giant, ancient tree with branches as far as the eye can see.

"How do you do that, Goldie?" Milo asks after finding his footing again. Goldie turns around and winks at him.

"It's a secret," she whispers before gesturing to the tree behind her. "Welcome to the Bank of Gnomes." Goldie steps out of the way, letting the twins take in the full magnificence of the tree.

The tree is so huge that you can't even see the top of the tree. The tree has hundreds of small windows and doors. Each window and door is unique and different from the other, much like the piggy bank Queen Penny is in charge of.

"I know the tree is very beautiful, but we don't have all day to admire it. Come on," Chip waves the twins closer and starts walking toward the tree. Milo and Mia jog to catch up with him.

"What exactly are we doing here?" Milo asks Chip. He turns around in a circle, trying to see everything at once.

"We are here to learn about banks, of course," Chip states, making it sound like the most logical thing in the world. Milo sighs at this, turning his attention to Goldie instead.

"Goldie, why do we need to learn about banks?" Milo tries again, this time with a different question.

Goldie hums a little tune under her breath before she answers. "Well, banks play a big part in money. There are many things we can use a bank for and many benefits of knowing how it works." She explains to Milo.

That makes sense to Milo. He doesn't know a lot about banks. He only knows that his mom and dad talk about going to the bank and having cards.

As they enter the bank, a kind-looking gnome walks up to them.

"Hello, hello everyone." She shakes their hands as she introduces herself. "I am Gilly, the bank manager here at Tree Finance." The gnome takes a step back and observes everyone.

"I am happy that you are here. Queen Penny called me to let me know you are on your way." Gilly folds her hands behind her back, her friendly expression turning more serious.

"She told me that you want to learn about banks and how they work." The twins nod their heads, yes, and Gilly continues. "If you have any questions, please ask me." Gilly turns around and starts walking.

The group of adventurers follows close to her, fascinated by everything going on around them. They come to a stop next to a window, looking into a big space filled with gnomes, counting coins.

"This is where we count the coins people put in their account. When they are done counting, they take a piece of paper next door." Gilly moves on to the next window. In this room, gnomes are writing things down in books and on computers.

"These gnomes write the number of coins down so that you can know how much money you have in your account." Gilly continues to talk as she moves on to the next part of their tour.

"Banks are a safe place for people to put their money that stops it from being stolen or lost. It is our job as the bank gnomes to make sure your money stays safe."

Milo raises his hand to ask Gilly a question.

"Yes, Milo?" Gilly stops walking, giving her full attention to Milo.

"How do you keep the money safe?" Milo wonders if they get superheroes to look after the money.

"We put the money in a big vault that only a few people can open," Gilly answers. "We make sure that the person taking money out of the bank is the same person that the money belongs to."

Satisfied that Milo understands the safety of the bank better, Gilly starts walking again. This time, they come to a stop in front of a standing screen. Gilly touches the screen, and it comes to life.

"There are two main accounts someone can open with the bank," Gilly explains to Milo and Mia.

"Accounts?" Mia asks, a bit confused.

"Accounts are the place and the way the bank keeps your money safe," Gilly answers. "You can have a savings account and a checking account."

Gilly touches a little money bag icon on the screen, and it opens to display two images. One was a little piggy bank, and the other was a little rectangular book.

"When you have a savings account, you use it to save your money. If you want, you can still use it to pay for things." Gilly tells the twins as she points to the piggy bank icon.

"A checking account is used when you want to buy things and pay more often. This is an account grownups usually have." Gilly explains as she points to the rectangular book icon.

"You need to get the account that works the best for your needs. Having the right account helps you manage your money responsibly." She said with a serious face. The twins watch as Gilly clicks on the piggy bank icon, and it opens a new page.

"You can open up your own savings account with the help of your parents." Gilly turns back to the twins. Goldie speaks up before Gilly continues with her lesson on banking.

"Do you want to open the savings account now?" Goldie asks the twins. They nod their heads enthusiastically. Goldie smiles at their excitement and takes a few steps to the left, giving herself some space to work.

Milo and Mia are captivated by what Goldie is doing as she conjures a blue and pink portal. It looks exactly like the one that brought the twins to the Land of Currency. Whatever it was that they expected, it was not to see their mom step out of it with a big smile on her face.

She greets the twins with hugs and gives Goldie and Chip a high-five. Their mom then turns to Gilly and surprises them once again.

"Hello, Gilly. It is so nice to see you." Gilly smiles brightly at the twins' mother and gives her a tight hug. They spend a few minutes catching up before Gilly turns serious again.

"Sasha, the twins want to open a savings account. Will you please help them?" Gilly asks their mother. She nods her head yes and moves over to the display screen. The next ten minutes are spent filling in some forms and the twins opening their own savings account with their mothers' help.

"Good," Gilly claps her hands together. "Now that you have the account, there is only one thing left to do."

Gilly looks at the twins, making sure she has their full attention.

"We need to deposit money into the account," Gilly informs the twins.

"What does deposit mean?" Milo asks.

"Deposit is when you put money into your account," Chip answers. Gilly nods her head at Chip's answer.

"Do you have any money you can deposit?" The twins look at each other before they show Gilly their piggy banks.

"We have some gold coins," Mia answers. "King Coin gave them to us, and Queen Penny gave us the piggy banks to keep it safe." Mia and Milo hand their piggy banks to Gilly.

"Thank you. Let's go deposit your money," Gilly turns around and walks back to the row of windows they looked at earlier. The twins jog to catch up with her.

"Will you please help Milo and Mia deposit their money into their account?" Gilly asks one of the gnomes behind the glass window. The gnome nods his head and takes the piggy bank from Gilly.

Mia and Milo look on as the gnomes count all their coins and make sure the money is all there. Next, they watch as the money is placed in the big vault.

"You can deposit into your account at any time. If you do it regularly, your savings will grow consistently." Gilly tells the twins. "When you leave your money in the savings account, you start earning interest."

Before either of the twins can ask Gilly what "interest" means, she continues talking.

"Interest is the bank's way of rewarding you for saving your money." Gilly pulls out a tablet from her pocket and shows the twins an animated video of money increasing.

"That is so cool!" Milo explained. "It's like my money is making money," Milo laughs, and everyone joins him.

"I need to go finish making dinner. I wish I could finish your adventure with you," the twin's mom tells them. "I am beyond proud of you two. You are growing up so fast." Goldie moves to the side and opens a portal for Milo and Mia's mom to return home as she says goodbye to everyone.

She pulls Milo and Mia in for a hug and says good-bye. Finally, after one last conversation with Gilly, their mom leaves. Milo and Mia wave as she steps through the portal and returns home.

Milo and Mia were very happy that their mother agreed to open a savings account for them. Mia can't wait to save for a new dress, and Milo is excited to see his money grow.

"Gilly," Mia calls out to get the gnomes' attention. Gilly looks up from her tablet, where she is busy working.

"If our money is in our savings account, how will we get it out when we need it?" Mia asks curiously, mixed with a bit of nervousness. She is afraid that once the money is in the account, she will never be able to use it.

"You can use your bank card or online banking to get your money again," Gilly explains, putting away her tablet and then turning to the closest window and calling for one of the gnomes.

"Will you please bring me Mia and Milo's bank card?" she asks the gnome. He nods his head and disappears into a room. It does not take long for him to return and hand two cards over to Gilly, one for Mia and the other for Milo.

To their delight, their bank cards match their piggy banks! Mia's card is pink and covered in glitter. Milo's card is green with blue stripes and even glows in the dark.

"When you want to pay for something, all you have to do is give them your bank card and the money will be taken from your account," Gilly explains to them that all they need to know about using their card.

"You each have a special pin for the card." Gilly shows them where to find their pins. "Don't share this pin with anyone. If someone has the pin, they can use your money." She warns them.

Gilly lowers her tablet so the twins can see the screen. "You can also ask your parents to help you see how much money you have in your account by using online banking." On the tablet, they can see their names, and under it, the number of gold coins they saved is displayed.

"This can help you stay on track with your saving goals," Gilly says with a proud smile. Anyone can see that Gilly enjoys working for the Gnome Bank.

"Thank you so much for showing us the bank." Mia thanks Gilly as she hugs her. Milo follows shortly with a hug of his own.

"Yeah," he agrees with his sister. "It is so cool that my money can make its own money," he says as he lets go of Gilly.

"It was my honor helping you two," Gilly answers with the biggest smile on her face. She turns to Goldie and Chip. "Thank you for bringing Mia and Milo to visit the bank. I hear you are going to do some planning next," Gilly says with a wink.

Learning with Milo and Mia.

Answer the questions below to see if you can remember what Gilly, the banker, taught us in this chapter. Choose one correct answer below.

<u>What account do you use to save your money?</u>

A. A checking account.
B. A savings account.
C. My Netflix account.

Why do we put money in the bank?

A. To keep it safe from being lost or stolen.

B. We don't; we put money in our socks.

C. Because it doesn't belong anywhere else.

What does it mean to deposit money into your bank account?

A. You take money out of your bank account.

B. You use your bank card to pay for something.

C. You put money into your bank account.

Ask yourself these questions and think about your answers.

1. Do you know anyone who has a bank card? What type of bank account do they have?

2. What does it mean to earn interest in your savings account?

Chapter 5

Market of Choices

G oldie creates another teleport, and everyone steps through it.

"How do you do that?" Milo asks, determined to get a straight answer out of Goldie, no matter how long it takes.

"A magician never reveals her secrets," Goldie answers him with a wink. Milo huffs in frustration, unsatisfied with her answer.

Milo and Mia make their way through the portal, with Goldie and Chip right behind them. The portal opens in a massive, bustling market. All around them are people and animals buying and selling things.

There were so many stalls that the twins could not see where the market ended. The market was filled with everything under the sun; if you can imagine it, you can buy it. There were vendors selling toys, clothes, food, and even some stalls where you could play games like ring toss.

Goldie has barely closed the portal when, out of nowhere, a bunny hops in front of them, blocking their way. "Hello, folks." He greets.

"Are you new to the market?" he asks, but before anyone can answer, he speaks again. "My name is Buddy, and I am a Budget Bunny." The bunny introduces himself while hopping in one place.

Mia follows Buddy's movement with her eyes, amazed that there can be so much energy in one person. Buddy looks at the group with expectant eyes, with a notebook and pen ready in his hands.

Milo looks at his sister in confusion, and Mia just shrugs her shoulder, also unsure what Buddy is waiting for.

"Where are we?" Milo asks. His question is directed at Goldie, but it is Buddy who answers him.

"Oh, you are in the Market of Choices, of course," he answers, dramatically waving his hands to show the market. "The place where you can get whatever you want or need." Buddy starts hopping in one place again. It seems like he can't stand still for too long.

"How many shops are there?" Mia asks, looking around at all the vendors. Buddy gives a snorting laugh.

"There are too many to count," Buddy says, giving a snorting laugh. "Believe me, I have tried. I am a numbers guy."

"Hello, Buddy," Goldie greets the energetic bunny. Buddy looks over at Goldie and gasps.

"Goldie! I didn't see you. When did you get here?" Goldie laughs lightly at Buddy, telling him that she was there the whole time.

"We came to the market to learn more about budgets. Will you please help us?" Goldie politely asks Buddy. His eyes widen, and he starts nodding his head enthusiastically.

"Yes, yes, yes." He chants, increasing the speed of his hops. "It will be an honor to show you guys around and teach you about budgeting." He takes each of the twin's hands in his and shakes them vigorously before letting go.

"Come on, there is no time to waste. Let's hop right to it." Buddy starts hopping away, and Milo and Mia scurry to catch up with his fast pace.

"Right," Buddy comes to a stop in front of a big poster with the words "Budget" and '50/30/20' on it.

"You know what it means to budget, right?" Buddy asks the twins. They shake their heads.

"I have never heard of budgeting before," says Mia.

"Oh, okay." Buddy was a little shocked at the idea of someone not knowing what budgeting was but pulled himself together rather quickly.

"Well, that is why you are here to learn." Buddy looks down at the notepad and pen in his hands. He takes two pieces of paper and gives one to each twin.

"I only have one pen, so you will have to share." Buddy hands the pen over to Mia and starts explaining what budgeting is.

"Budgeting is having a plan for your money. How much you have, how much you can spend, and how much you want to save." Buddy is standing still; talking about budgeting always makes him calm.

"You can spend your money on things you need. That will be things that are essential for living, like food and water." Buddy explains to the Twins.

"Wants, on the other hand, are things you like, but they aren't necessary. Think of things like candy and toys. They are nice to have, but we don't need them to survive." He continues.

"There are many ways you can budget, but I have found that the 50/30/20 rule works the best." Buddy points to the poster behind him.

"You take your allowance and use 50% of it for the things you need, 30% for the things you want, and 20% you put away for savings." Buddie sees the uncertainty on their faces and decides to take a different approach.

"Think of it as a pie-half goes to needs, a smaller piece to wants, and the rest for saving."

Buddy points down to the paper they have, "Write your allowance on the top of the paper. After that, quickly make a list by putting your needs on one side and your wants on the other." The twins do as Buddy instructs them.

Both of them hope that they are doing it right. When they are done, they give him their lists. He nods his head, happy with their work.

"Mr. Buddy," Mia raises her hand. "Why do we divide it into 50, 30, and 20?" Mia asks Buddy her question. Milo is the one who is strong in numbers. Buddy starts hopping with excitement because of Mia's question. He loves questions almost as much as he loves numbers and helping people budget.

"When you count everything together, you get 100." Mia frowns at Buddy, not understanding what he is trying to say.

"Think of it like this: your entire allowance is $100. We need to use $50 of the hundred for the things you need, $30 for what you want, and $20 you save." Buddy smiles at the understanding that enters Mia's eyes.

Buddy reaches into a pouch that is hanging over his shoulder. He pulls out some paper money and hands it to the twins.

"Now that you know how to budget for things, walk around the market and buy something that is a need and something that is a want," Buddy instructs the twins.

"Remember what we learned about needs and wants. I will come with you, but I won't give you any guidance. I want to see how you do in a real-life situation." Milo and Mia look at each other with excitement. They don't get a lot of opportunities to buy things on their own.

With the help from everyone so far, the twins under-stand money better, and they can't wait to start using their knowledge. Milo and Mia take the lead as they start exploring the market, looking for things they can spend their money on.

The twins stop at every stall they come across, ad-miring everything. The lovely smell of food enticed them to stop at the next stall. Milo's mouth is watering as they watch the vendor make a sandwich.

"That looks so yummy," Milo says, captivated by the scene in front of him. Mia steps closer, curious to see what caught her brother's attention.

"That does look good," Mia agrees with her brother. She turns to Buddy to ask him a question.

"Does food count as a need, Buddy?" Milo breaks eye contact with the delicious-looking sandwich and looks at Buddy, waiting for his answer to Mia's question.

"Let's think about it together. A sandwich is a food; does food count as a need or a want?" Buddy turns the question back to Mia. Mia looks at her brother and con-templates Buddy's question.

Food is necessary for survival, so a sandwich is a need! Mia smiles at her twin. "We can get sandwiches;

eating food is a need." Excited, they order a sandwich and wait in anticipation for it. The first bite of the sandwich is the best.

Mia takes her time to eat her sandwich. She takes small bites and chews slowly. Milo, on the other hand, inhales the sandwich, barely breathing in between the bites. When Milo is done with his sandwich, he licks his fingers clean and starts looking around the market, looking for something.

"What are you looking for, Milo?" Chip comes to stand next to him and starts looking around the market as well, joining Milo in his search.

"I'm looking for something to drink," Milo tells Chip, not taking his eyes off the bustling market. When Mia was done eating, the group started walking again, and this time, they were looking for something to drink.

As they passed the stalls, the vendors were trying to catch their attention and convince the twins to buy their products. Milo and Mia stopped a few times to look at the things being sold, but Goldie reminded them that they were looking for something to drink first.

Finally, after what felt like an eternity, the twins found a stall selling all kinds of things to drink. The vendor had water, juice, and even fizzy pop. Milo was reaching for an apple juice when his sister reminded him of their instructions.

"We need to buy things for our needs first, like water. If we buy the juice, it will count as something we want." With a frown, Milo considers this before deciding to take a bottle of water, even if he really wants apple juice.

Buddy looked at the exchange between the siblings and smiled to himself, happy to see the twins were starting to learn the difference between needs and wants. They are making him proud. No longer hungry or thirsty, the twins walk through the market at a leisurely pace; they want to enjoy the atmosphere of the market before they leave.

As they are walking around, Milo spots a toy table filled with different models of toy cars. Excitedly, he runs over to the table. He looks over every single toy car. Some he already has back at home, but there are many he still needs for his collection.

And then it happens. Milo spots the perfect car. He has been looking for this car everywhere but hasn't had any luck until today. The toy car is painted a beautiful, deep red color with gold parts scattered around the body of the toy car.

"Hello, sir," Milo greets the toy car vendor. "Will you please hand me that car over there?" Milo asks the vendor as he points to the red toy car he wants. The vendor hands the toy car to Milo, and Milo instantly falls in love with it. With bright eyes, he asks the vendor what the price is for the red toy car.

To Milo's disappointment, the toy car is outside his budget. If he buys the toy car now, he will have to use some of the money he wants to save. Milo looks at the toy car he wants and at the budget he has created with the help of Buddy. He desperately wants the car, but he knows how important it is to save his money.

Milo gives the toy car back to the vendor and thanks him. He walks away from the toy table with a plan already forming in his head. He will save his money and come and buy the car in a few months when he has enough.

"Why didn't you get the car?" Mia asks her brother when he gets back without it.

"I decided to save some money before I buy it," Milo answers his sister. "Have you found anything you want?"

Mia looks down at her shoes; her lower lip pouted slightly. "I found a beautiful necklace that looks just like the one mom has, but I don't have enough money." Milo pulls his sister into a tight hug.

"It's okay, Mia; you can also save your money and buy it later." Mia wipes away a few tears that escape and nods her head at Milo. "Okay."

"Buddy, can we walk around the market a little longer even if we don't buy anything?" Milo asks Buddy after making sure Mia is okay.

"Of course you can," Buddy says with a smile.

Together, the group walks around the market, enjoying the lovely atmosphere and friendly people. The twins walked from one stall to the next, admiring all the beautifully crafted things.

On their exploration of the market, they found a stall filled with all types of games. The stall had every form of card and board game you could think of. The twins looked through every game until they found one that they both liked.

They called the vendor over and asked her how much the game was. To their disappointment, the game was outside their budgets.

"Milo," Mia turns to her brother. "Do you want to buy a board game with me?" she asks him.

"We will both be playing with it, so it just makes sense that we put our money together to buy it." Milo agrees immediately, excited to buy something. The twins put their money together and buy a board game that they can play by themselves or even with their parents.

"That was a wonderful idea, Mia." Buddy praises her. "I can see that you both understand the importance of budgeting better now." Milo and Mia nod their heads at Buddy's statement.

"Remember, choosing needs first and saving a little each time is how you stick to your budget and still get what you want someday." Buddy gives them one last reminder.

"It is about time we get going," Goldie speaks up.

The twins wave goodbye to Buddy as he hops off to help someone else set up a budget that works.

"Next stop, Wise Owl's Shop," Chip says excitedly as Goldie opens a portal.

Learning with Milo and Mia.

Answer the questions below to see if you can remember what Buddy taught us in this chapter. Choose one correct answer below.

What does it mean when something is a need?

A. It is when you go to the park for a picnic.

B. Something fun to do with your friends.

C. It is something you need to survive, like food and water.

Identify all the wants in the list below.

A. Saving your money in a piggy bank.

B. Water, sandwiches, school supplies.

C. Toys, candy, a new coloring book.

Why did Milo and Mia not buy the toy car and necklace?

A. It was too expensive and didn't fit into their budget.

B. They didn't want it anymore.

C. They remembered they already had a toy car and necklace at home.

Ask yourself these questions and think about your answers.

1. Can you think of a need and a want in your life?

2. What would you do if you wanted to buy something but didn't have enough money in your budget?

Chapter 6

Abundance of Deals

By now, Milo and Mia are getting used to going through the portals Goldie makes for them. This time, the portal leads them to a cozy shop with warm lights and an inviting atmosphere. The shop is filled from floor to ceiling with all kinds of interesting things. There are brightly colored stickers with numbers on them.

"Oh wow, this place hasn't changed at all since the last time we were here." Comments Chip as he looks around the room. Goldie nods her head, steps towards a counter, and rings the bell.

"You know Ollie likes keeping things the same; he has a place for everything." Just as Goldie stops talking, they hear a hoot followed by a shuffling of feet somewhere in the shop.

"I'm coming," a voice calls out, followed by another hoot. Chip steps forward and stands next to Goldie. He starts ringing the bell excessively and laughs as he does so. He only manages to do it three times before Goldie catches his hand and stops him.

"You never let me have any fun," Chip pouts at her.

"You know Ollie dislikes it when people ring the bell more than once." Goldie scolds Chip with a stern voice, but Chip just smiles at her.

"I know. That's why I do it." Chip tells Goldie confidently. Before they can start arguing, a loud hoot interrupts them, and an old Owl steps out from behind a stack of boxes. The owl is a beautiful dust-brown color and is wearing gold glasses. The feathers on top of his head are sticking out in all directions, making it look like he just got out of bed.

"I should have known it was you two," hooted the owl with a shake of his head. He turns his attention away from Goldie and Chip and rests his eyes on the twins. He gives them a big smile and nods his head in greeting.

"Hello, little ones. I am Ollie."

"Hello, Ollie," the twins greet him back at the same time. Ollie lets out a belly laugh filled with hoots at their greeting, delighted by the way they are connected with each other.

"What brings you to my shop today?" Ollie asks as he looks between the twins and Chip. Goldie clears her throat and steps forward.

"We were wondering if you would be willing to teach Milo and Mia about looking for deals." Ollie's eyes roam over Goldie's face; he gives her a wink and nods his head.

"I would be delighted to teach these young ones. Come this way." Ollie gestures with his wing, and everyone follows him. They don't walk long before they come to a stop.

"Welcome to my shop, a place where you will find an abundance of deals!" Ollie said with flair as he spun in a circle.

"I am the master of all deals, and today, I will be teaching you my craft." Milo and Mia share a look, but they are not sure what to expect.

"Just like we can save money in our bank accounts and through budgeting, we can also save money by looking for deals and comparing prices," Ollie said in his wise owl voice.

"Some shops sell the same thing, but their prices might be different from each other." Ollie turns around and reaches into a random box behind him. He pulls out a piece of paper and a bag of coins. He turns back around and hands Milo and Mia a paper. Ollie then opened the bag and pulled out eight gold coins, giving each twin four coins.

"Right," Ollie claps his wings together. "I want you to go around the shop and find every item on your list at the best price possible." Milo and Mia compare their list and notice that they are not the same.

"Do you want to work together, Mia?" Milo asks his sister as he looks at his list, feeling a little overwhelmed at the task before him. Mia looks at her brother and sees the uncertainty in his eyes. She nods her head and puts her own list in her pocket.

"Yeah. We can work on both lists at the same time." Milo nods his head in agreement, and the twins set off to find the things on their list.

The first thing they need to find is a bottle of dishwashing liquid. The twins walk around and find the table with cleaning supplies on it.

"Look, Mia, this table has the dishwashing liquid on it." Milo points to the table. Mia walks closer and looks at the dishwashing liquid.

"It cost one entire gold coin, Milo. Ollie said that we need to look around and try to find the best price for the items on our list." Milo nods his head in agreement, and they continue their search.

It does not take them long to find another table selling cleaning supplies, and this time, the dishwashing liquid is only three silver coins. On the same table, they found some washing gloves that Mia needed to find for her list, also for only three silver coins.

And so the twins went all around Ollie's shop, looking for the best deal they could find. The more they looked out for deals, the more they were able to find something that would save them money.

Mia was standing in front of a table filled with cookies and other baked goods, with two different boxes of cookies in her hand. She frowns down at the boxes, not sure which one she should choose. They both look the same and have the exact same price.

Ollie sees Mia's struggle and walks closer to her. He touches her shoulder lightly to get her attention. "Is there something I can help you with?" Ollie asks Mia.

She looks up at the wise old owl, grateful for the help he is offering her.

"I need to buy a box of cookies, but I can't decide between these two boxes. They cost the same." Mia shows her two choices to Ollie. He takes the two cookie boxes from her and looks at them closely. With a frustrated hoot, he reaches into the bag around his waist and removes a pair of glasses, putting it on.

After looking at the boxes for a few moments, he hands both boxes back to Mia and removes his glasses.

"Mia, I want you to look at the boxes and tell me if you see anything different between them." Mia frowns up at Ollie, not sure why she has to read the box but doing it anyway. Her eyes scan over the boxes, trying to find the difference.

On the front of the boxes, she can see that the company that makes the cookies is different, and the pictures they are using are also different. Mia turns the boxes around and starts reading the labels.

The first box of cookies has more sugar in it than the second box. Happy with her finds, Mia tells Ollie about everything she found.

"On the front of the boxes, the company name and the picture used for the cookies are different. And this box has more sugar than this one." Mia shows the differences to Ollie. The wise owl looks at everything she is showing him and nods his head, along with her explanation.

"You did a wonderful job, Mia. There is one more thing that is different between the two boxes." Ollie gives Mia a moment to see if she can spot the difference.

"Look at how much they weigh," Ollie gives Mia a clue when she could not find the last difference.

"Look," With a gasp, Mia finds it and excitedly points it out. "The box with more sugar only has ten cookies in it. This box has twelve!" Mia holds up the box of cookies in the air. Ollie hoots in excitement with her and gives her praise for finding the difference.

"Sometimes things may cost the same and even look the same. But the amount you get is different." Ollie said wisely.

"As a smart shopper, we need to not only look at the prices but also make sure that the amount we are getting is worth the price." Mia thanks Ollie for showing her what to look for. Excited that she learned something new, Mia ran over to her brother, who was looking at a selection of bread at another stall.

Mia tells him how to look for the weight or quality of something to see if you are getting a good deal.

"Which one would be better to buy," Milo asks his sister, pointing to the selection of bread in front of them. Mia steps closer, and together, the twins go through everything until they find the best deal.

"This one is the best," Mia tells her brother. "It cost the same as all the other breads, but it has seeds in it, and you get two slices more." Milo takes the bread from Mia and pays for it, thanking the vendor for his patience.

With more information on how not to look for good deals, Mia and Milo set out to find the rest of the things on their list.

"Mia," Milo calls out to his sister on the other side of the room. "Why don't we make it a race? The first one to get all their things and save the most money wins." Milo smiles brightly at his sister. Not one to ever back down from a challenge, Mia agrees.

Goldie plays the referee and lays down some rules. When she is satisfied with the twins agreeing to her rules, she counts them down.

"Three, two, one. Go!" Milo and Mia jump right into the action, running in opposite directions to finish their lists. The twins have different methods to be the ultimate smart savers.

Mia is going to multiple stalls and double-checking all prices to ensure she gets the best deal for the items individually. This is taking a little longer, but it ensures that she is saving as much money as she possibly can.

Milo is taking a different approach. He is looking out for bundle deals on his items as much as he can. This means that he is getting through his list faster and saving money on two items at the same time. The savings for the individual items might not be the best, but because he is buying them together, the combined savings are still good.

Out of breath, Milo and Mia arrive at the same stall. Both the twins only have one item left on their list. They need to buy a book. The only problem is that no matter how hard they look, neither one of the two can find a good deal for a book.

The twins have an intense stare-down, trying to intimidate each other. They are having a silent conversation that no one else understands but them. Ollie sees the tension rising between the siblings and decides to step in.

"Let me take a look at your list." He extends his wings and waits for the twins to hand over their list. Milo and Mia reluctantly break eye contact and hand their lists over to Ollie.

The wise owl studies their lists with a smile, happy to see that they were able to get almost everything.

"I see you guys only need one more item each and have been saving quite a bit of money with your purchases today." Ollie shares his observation.

"There is one more smart saver trick I can teach you that will help you with this last item on the list." Ollie smiles at the twins. Milo and Mia give their full attention to Ollie, eager to learn more about finding good deals.

Ollie starts walking, and the twins follow him. He comes to a stop in front of a table that has a big sign on it.

"Milo, can you tell me what this sign says?" Ollie points to the red sign on the table.

"It says, Sale 50% off." Milo reads the sign.

"Good, and what does this mean?" Ollie asks Mia.

"Does it mean that everything on this table is 50% off?" Mia asks Ollie.

"Bravo!" Ollie cheers. "That's correct, Mia. Everything on this table is half-price. Often, stores will have sales like this on items they want to get rid of. This is another brilliant way to save money and be a smart shopper."

The twins turn back to the table and notice there are two books on sale. They each take a book and finish their list.

The twins show their list to Ollie one more time and hand over the money they have left. Ollie is really impressed with the two young children. He has given this challenge to many people before, but no one has been able to save as much money as the twins.

"It is my honor to present you two with this." Ollie reaches into the bag around his waist and pulls out two pins. He gives one pin to Milo and one to Mia.

"As proof that you are smart shoppers, accept these pins and wear them with pride." Milo and Mia smile at Ollie, ecstatic to have received the Smart Shopper pin from Ollie.

Milo and Mia give Ollie a tight hug and thank him for all his help. They can't wait to use their smart shopper skills.

They say goodbye to Ollie, and he thanks them for visiting, reminding them that being a smart shopper is a valuable skill.

Learning with Milo and Mia.

Answer the questions below to see if you can remember what Goldie and Chip taught us in this chapter. Choose one correct answer below.

<u>Why is it important to be a smart shopper?</u>

    A. It helps us save money.
    B. It is fun to go to different stores.
    C. We can spend more time shopping.

What are some ways you can be a smart shopper?

A. By wearing nice shoes when you go shopping.

B. You can be friendly to the cashier who is helping you.

C. You can compare prices and quantities of products.

Why should you look at the label when you buy things?

A. There are jokes written on it.

B. It has important information like ingredients and weight/quantity.

C. It can tell you what you should buy next.

Ask yourself these questions and think about your answers.

1. Why is it important to think carefully before spending your money?

2. Do you see sale signs when you go shopping?

Chapter 7

Time to Work

This time, instead of Goldie creating a portal, they walked all the way from Ollie's shop to a big hill. Standing at the bottom of the hill, the twins look up, squinting as they try to see what is happening on top of the hill.

"Where are we going next?" Milo asks Goldie as he looks around, trying to see if there is anything else close to them besides the massive hill. Goldie smiles at him and says nothing, only pointing up the hill.

"Up there?" Milo asks in disbelief. Goldie nods her head, and Milo groans in disappointment. So, the group sets out to climb the giant hill.

Milo and Mia are out of breath when they finally reach the top. Milo dramatically drops to the ground and lies on his back, putting his arm over his eyes.

"Go on without me," he said in a muffled voice. "I will stay here and die in peace." Mia rolls her eyes at Milo's dramatic antics and walks over to him. She takes him by his hand and pulls him up.

"Stop being so dramatic, Milo; it was not that bad." Milo sticks his tongue out at his sister and turns his attention to the clearing in front of him.

"What is this place?" he asks under his breath, dusting off his clothes.

"Welcome to the District of Jobs," Chips announces with a flair.

"Why are we at the District of Jobs?" Mia asks Goldie, confused. They walk over to the entrance as Goldie answers Mia.

"You have been learning about how to work with money responsibly, and now it is time that you two learn where money comes from." They stop at the entrance of the District of Jobs and are greeted by a friendly young man in a work uniform.

"Welcome to the District of Jobs. My name is Jaxon; how can I serve you today?" Jaxon greets them with a smile. Goldie steps forward and shakes Jaxon's hand.

"It is lovely to finally meet you, Jaxon. I am Goldie, and this is my partner, Chip." Chip steps forward and shakes Jaxon's hand as well.

"Will you please show these two around the District of Jobs and let them try out a few?" Jaxon looks over at the twins after Goldie has pointed them out. He assesses them with his eyes and turns back to Goldie.

"It would be my pleasure. Just leave them with me, and they will learn the importance of working hard." Goldie nudges the twins in Jaxon's direction and steps back.

"You will be doing this part alone. Chip and I will see you when you are done. Good luck." Chip and Goldie wave goodbye as Jaxon leads the twins into the District of Jobs.

The air is filled with the sound of tools, laughter, and music as people go about doing their jobs. Jaxon seems to be popular, as many people greet him as they walk past.

"The District of Jobs is where people use their skills and passions to deliver goods and services in exchange for money," Jaxon explains as they walk past a young woman selling freshly baked bread.

"Some people are good with their hands, so they do things like construction or making furniture." Jaxon points to the left of them, where a group of men and women are building a new office.

"Other people are talented at singing and dancing, so they entertain people." They walk past a seating area where people are eating and relaxing as they watch two people on stage dance to a high-energy song.

"There are many jobs out there you can do. Why don't we start here?" Jaxon leads them into a cozy-looking bakery. He greets the person attending the till with a smile and a wave before he leads the twins to the back.

"This is Russell, the best baker in the district. You will be helping him make his next batch of bread."

Rupert turns to the kids and cleans his hands with a kitchen towel he had in the back pocket of his pants.

"Go wash your hands and put on an apron." He points to the back of the kitchen, where a big sink is. The twins do as they are instructed. When they return to Rupert, he hands them each a hairnet and shows them how to put it on.

"Every job has a uniform; this is mine," Rupert tells the twins. He turns back to his working bench and splits the dough he is working on into three pieces. He then proceeds to show the twins how to knead the dough and shape buns.

The twins work in silence with Rupert, enjoying the calming nature of the work. Once they are done, Rupert inspects their rolls and gives them a thumbs up.

"These look good. Go to the front and get your money from the lady at the cash register." Rupert said in a gruff voice. He picks up the baking tray where they placed the rolls and walks over to the oven, putting the rolls in.

Milo and Mia thank Rupert for teaching them how to knead dough and make bread rolls. Just as they receive their money from the nice lady behind the counter, Jaxon walks into the bakery.

"How was it?" He asks the twins.

"It was boring," Milo complains as they walk out of the bakery.

"I loved it," Mia interrupted her brother, complaining. "It was so relaxing to knead the dough. It made me feel calm." Jaxon laughed at the different reactions the twins had to working in the bakery.

"Why are we at the construction site?" Mia asks as they come to a stop in front of their next work assignment.

"We will be helping the builders with this building." Jaxon guides them to a bench filled with yellow hats, orange vests, and big goggles.

"Put these on." Jaxon hands the twins one of each thing on the table. "It is very important to wear safety gear when you do jobs like construction because you can get really hurt if you don't wear them." Milo and Mia put on their safety gear and followed Jaxon again.

They first walk over to a very stern-looking man with a big blue paper in his hands.

"This is the architect; he makes sure that the building is being built according to the blueprint."

They walk over to the architect and learn how to draw a blueprint and make measurements. Next, they move on to the foreman of the building site. He is the guy that makes sure the construction gets done.

The foreman is a big guy with a no-nonsense facial expression who takes his job very seriously.

"I have to make sure that everyone on the construction site knows what they need to do and does it right," the foreman explains as he shows them around the site. He walks with a clipboard in his hands and an extra-hard hat tied to his belt.

The foreman leads them to a group of construction workers busy working on something. "You will be helping these fine men lay this foundation. When you are done, come and find me." And just like that, the foreman walks away and leaves the twins with the construction workers.

Excited to get started, Milo walks over to one of the men and asks him how they can help. Milo and Mia spend the next twenty minutes assisting the kind construction workers by carrying around their tools and handing them the ones they need.

When they are done, they find the foreman, and he gives them some gold coins, thanking the twins for their hard work. Jaxon is there, waiting for them.

"I loved doing construction work!" Milo exclaims as soon as he sees Jaxon, who laughs at the change in the young boy. Milo spends the trip to their next destination talking about how much he enjoyed working with his hands.

They walk into an open-air studio with some people covered in paint and clay. Jaxon walks over to an older woman with gray hair and a paint streak on her left cheek.

"Jaxon, oh, how lovely it is to see you again!" The lady walks over to Jaxon and gives him one kiss on each cheek.

"It is good to see you, Maggie. This is Milo and Mia." Jaxon greets her and introduces the twins. Maggie leads them deeper into the studio and to a pair of canvases. Maggie shows them all the paints and paintbrushes.

"Here are your canvases. You can paint whatever you want too. When you are done, we will display them with the rest, and if someone buys your art, you get to keep the money." Maggie spends some time with the twins, teaching them different painting techniques and how to work with colors.

The twins each make two beautiful paintings. Mia made two paintings about nature and animals, where Milo painted brave nights fighting dragons and saving princesses. Next, they moved to the pottery station, where a nice young man taught them how to make sculptures using clay.

The twins had a lot of fun making art with all kinds of different people. When Jaxon came to get them, they were covered in paint, clay, and even some glitter after having a glitter fight.

"It looks like you two had a lot of fun," Jaxon laughs as he dusts off Milo's head, which is full of glitter.

For their final job of the day, Jaxon takes them to the entertainment center in the middle of the District of Jobs. Here, he introduces them to a funny-looking man.

"Milo, Mia, this is Gavin. He is the head of entertainment here in the district." Gavin waves at the twins and shakes Jaxon's hand.

"Come on, we don't have much time. I still need to teach you the choreography about the dance number." Gavin leads the twins backstage and introduces them to the dancing team. Milo and Mia have a lot of fun as they learn to dance.

Gavin is impressed with how fast they are catching up, so he decides to teach them the song, too. When the twins are done learning the words to the song, they get to put on their costumes, and their faces get painted as well.

"I'm nervous," Milo whispers to Mia as they stand on stage, waiting for the curtains to rise and their performance to start.

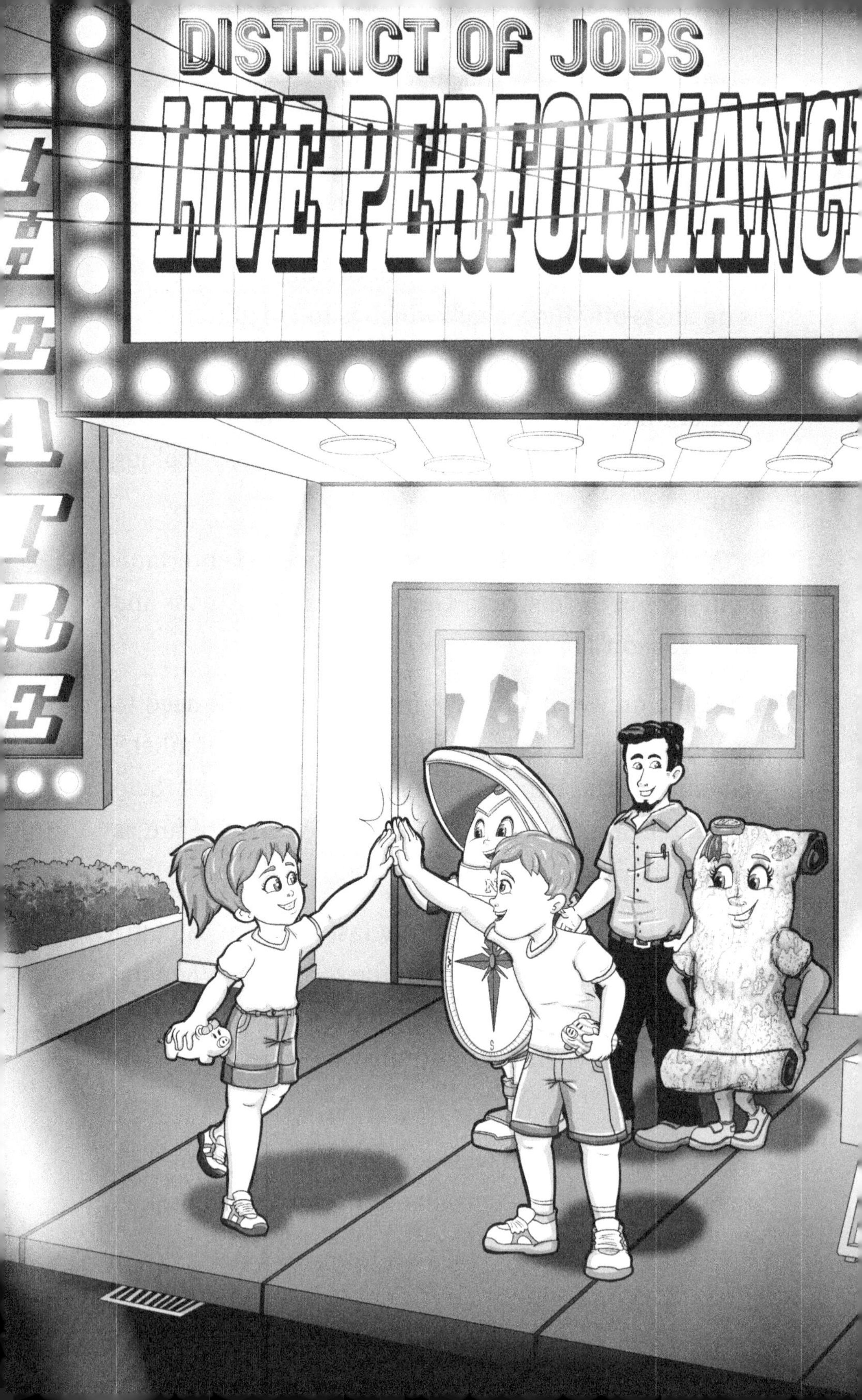
DISTRICT OF JOBS
LIVE PERFORMANC
THEATRE

"Me too," she whispers back as the curtain rises.

Milo and Mia's performance goes well, and they get a standing ovation from the crowd. After the performance, they are gathered behind the stage with the dance team, getting well-done pats on the shoulders. Gavin comes around and pays everyone for the hard work they did.

Milo and Mia put the money into their piggy banks. They have been working hard the entire day, and the feeling of getting paid for the work they put in is very rewarding.

Jaxon comes to get them, and to their delight, Goldie and Chip are with him.

"We saw your performance." Chip jumps up and down after giving the twins a high-five. "You guys were so cool up there!" The twins beam at him.

"You did very well today," Jaxon compliments them. "You worked hard no matter the job you did, and that is something to be proud of." The twins turn to each other with bright smiles; they really enjoy earning money.

"It is important to remember that there are always opportunities to learn something new and to try different jobs. You can turn your passion into a paying job if you work hard enough at it."

Jaxon says goodbye to the twins after sharing his wise words, saying he needs to return to his own work.

Milo and Mia can't stop talking as they walk with Goldie and Chip out of the District of Jobs.

"My favorite part was helping the baker make his bread. It was so relaxing to knead the bread and put it into the oven," Mia said with a content sigh while Milo stuck his tongue out at his sister.

"That was so boring," Milo teased Mia with a smile. "I really enjoyed going to the construction site with all the strong men." Milo flexes his arms.

Goldie and Chip laugh at this; they have missed the twins while they are learning about jobs and working hard.

"Now that you know how to make money and how to save it, you need to learn how to make it grow," Goldie tells the twins as she opens a portal to their next destination.

Learning with Milo and Mia.

Answer the questions below to see if you can remember what Jaxon taught us in this chapter. Choose one correct answer below.

Why do you need to wear a uniform when you do certain jobs?

A. It helps people recognize what you do, like being a police officer.

B. It is fun to do.

C. So we can spend more time looking at ourselves in the mirror.

What are some ways a construction worker keeps themselves safe?

A. By wearing nice shoes with lights in them.

B. They wear a hard hat and a reflective jacket.

C. They wear funny pants with polka dots on them.

Do you get paid when you work hard?

A. No, you just work hard for no reason.

B. Maybe, but only if you ask your parents to pay you.

C. Yes, you do get paid.

Ask yourself these questions and think about your answers.

1. What are some jobs you think you would enjoy doing?

2. Why is it important to work hard at the jobs we do?

Chapter 8

Garden of Growth

The portal opens in a lush garden with green grass ad trees as far as the eye can see. The twins step out of the portal and gasp, mesmerized by the sight before them. Every time they think they have seen all the Land of Currency has to offer, they find something new to marvel at.

"Wow, it is so pretty here." Mia turns in a slow circle as she tries to take everything in. "Where are we, Goldie?" Mia's eyes run over all the plants in the garden; a beautiful pink flower catches her attention. She walks closer to inspect it; she has never seen a flower like this before.

"We are in the Garden of Growth," Goldie answers her. Mia slowly stretches out her hand to pluck the beautiful pink flower in front of her. She wants to take it home and show it to her grandmother. The garden is truly magical; all the flowers and trees have a soft glow.

"I wouldn't do that if I were you." A bell-like voice sounds behind Mia. "It is not yours to harvest."

Mia turns around but can't find the source of the voice. Was it her imagination speaking to her? There is a soft touch on Mia's shoulder, and she turns to her left.

There, flying in front of her face is a fairy! Mia stumbles back a little in surprise.

"Oh, I'm sorry. I didn't mean to frighten you," the fairy speaks in the bell-like voice Mia had heard earlier. She has no words as she watches the fairy fly over to Goldie and Chip.

"How lovely it is to see you two again. It has been ages." The fairy gives a hug to Goldie and Chip before she turns back to Milo and Mia.

"My name is Ivy, and I am the head investment fairy here in the Garden of Growth." Ivy does a little curtsy to the twins after introducing herself.

"My name is Milo, and this is my twin sister, Mia," Milo speaks up. He had been quiet since they entered the Garden of Growth, distracted by all the strange plants he'd never seen before.

"Are you a real fairy?" Mia asks Ivy.

Ivy gives a little tinkling laugh, "Yes, Mia. I am a real fairy."

"What is this place?" Milo asks Ivy as his eyes sweep over the garden around them. Ivy gives him a toothy smile, delighted by his curiosity.

"This place is known as the Garden of Growth." Ivy flies around them in a circle before stooping in front of them again.

"Here, your money can grow, just like plants and trees," Ivy tells the twins. Mia looks at the plants and trees around them with new eyes. The pink flower she found so beautiful catches her attention again.

"Does that mean that the plants and trees are other people's money that has grown?" Mia asks Ivy.

"Yes, Mia," Ivy answers Mia and flies ahead of the group. "Follow me, and I will show you the many plants we have growing in the garden." The twins, along with Goldie and Chip, follow after Ivy. She comes to a stop in a plantation filled with different-sized trees.

A cloud of pink glitter covers Ivy. When the cloud clears, she is standing on her two feet, roughly the same size as the twins. Milo blinks a few times and rubs his eyes with his hands, shocked by what he just saw. He turns to Mia and sees that she is just as surprised as he is.

"Investing money is like planting a seed. When you take care of the seed and give it enough water and sunlight, it will turn into a beautiful tree or plant over time." Ivy starts to walk slowly, and the twins follow her.

"Just like plants, some investments grow faster than others." They walk past a forest filled with many different trees, not one the same height as the others.

"When we invest money, we can do it safely, but the investment will grow slowly." They stop in front of a big oak tree. Ivy lovingly strokes the base of the tree.

"This investment has been growing for over 30 years." Ivy looks up at the tree, and the twins follow her lead. They can barely see the top of the tree.

"This investment is sure and strong; even when the weather is bad, the tree will stay standing. This is what makes the investment safe. Even if something bad were to happen in the market, the owner of the tree will not lose their investment." Ivy informs them with a tilt of her head.

They move on to a field filled with many exotic-looking flowers; some flowers are vibrant in color, while others are starting to die.

"You can also choose to invest your money into things that carry more risk. Your investment will grow fast, but unlike the oak tree, these flowers need very special conditions to grow. Otherwise, they will die." Ivy explains as they walk past a row of dying flowers.

"It is important to remember that even if you invest your money, whether in high-risk or low-risk profiles, you still need to be responsible with it." Ivy hands a watering can to the twins, and together, they water the exotic flowers.

After watering all the exotic flowers, they walk to the end of the garden, where they find an area filled with beautiful green plants. Ivy walks by the plants and whispers words of encouragement to help them grow.

"Then there are investment options like these wonderful plants here. They need a bit more attention than the oak tree to grow, but they are not as needy as the exotic flowers." Green light comes from Ivy's fingers as she touches a torn leaf of a plant. The plant is restored, and Ivy moves on.

"This is what we call a moderate-risk investment."

They move on from the flower garden to a wide-open field. Unlike the previous plantations the twins have seen, this field is filled with lots of different trees and flowers, all planted in neat rows. Some of them grow slowly, like oak, while others grow fast, like exotic flowers.

"Now we are starting to get to the fun stuff," Ivy says as she excitedly claps her hands. She walks over to what looks like a ticket booth in the middle of the garden. Once at the window, she calls Milo and Mia to join her.

"Will you please hand me some of the coins you got for working in the District of Jobs?" Ivy holds her hand out to the twins. Mia reaches into her bag without any second thought and hands it over to Ivy. Milo, on the other hand, is a bit slower in handing his hard-earned money over.

"I know it is hard to invest money," Ivy sympathizes with Milo. "Investing might take time, but the reward is worth the wait, I promise." Milo looks at Ivy and then at his sister. Mia gives him a reassuring smile.

"Come on, Milo. We said we wanted to learn about money; this is just another part of it." Mia encourages her brother. Milo looks down at the money in his hand before giving it to Ivy.

Ivy thanks Milo and turns to the booth window.

"Can we please exchange this for some money seeds?" The fairy in the booth nods her head yes and opens a drawer with many different seeds in it.

"What money seeds would you like?" The fairy asks Ivy.

"Can we please get a little bit of everything?" Ivy answers the fairy.

After getting all the seeds and saying thank you, Ivy turns back to the twins.

"Here you go." She hands them each a bag of seeds with a smile.

"Why don't we go plant some seeds and invest some money?" Ivy points to the garden filled with different plants they were just in.

The twins walk with Ivy and discuss what they will be doing with their money seeds.

"I am going to put all my money seeds in the high-risk investment," Milo tells his sister with a wide smile. "I want to make as much money as soon as possible."

"I don't think that is a good idea, Milo," Mia argues with her brother. "What if you lose all your money?"

"I have decided to put everything into the low-risk investment. It is better to wait for the money and know you will get it than lose it all." Mia tells Milo with her nose in the air. Soon, the twins are arguing about what investment would be the best.

"I hate to break it to you, but you both are wrong," Ivy decides to interrupt the twin's argument before it gets too heated. Milo and Mia turn to Ivy, both frowning at her.

"To have an investment profile that is just risky or just safe won't give you the best results," Ivy tells the twins with a smile, happy to be able to teach them.

"You need to have a diverse profile that balances the risks and rewards. That means you have a mix of safe, moderate, and risky investments." Ivy leads the twins over to the first group of plants; together, they see what safe investments look like and move on.

Just as Ivy helped the twins choose safe investments, she also guided them to choose moderate and risky investments. As they choose, Ivy gives all the pros and cons to the twins so that they can make good decisions.

"Before you decide on any investment, you must always do some research first. This will help you make an informed decision and know what to expect." Ivy leads the twins to a big screen a few yards from the booth where they got their money seeds earlier.

"This will show us how your seeds will grow and what they might look like at the end of your investment period." Ivy touches the screen, and it splits in two.

Milo's name was displayed on top of the screen on the left side, and Mia's was displayed on the right side. The twins watched as an animation started playing on the screen. The twins have two different investment profiles, but they are both balanced.

Milo has a bit more moderate and risky investments. His side of the screen springs to life fast, but there are some plants that die just as fast as they sprouted.

"Those are your high-risk, high-reward investments," Ivy tells Milo as she pauses the animation.

They move on to Mia's investments next after Ivy presses a few buttons on the screen. Mia's investment profile has more safe investments. This means that her plants are growing slower, but there are fewer plants that are dying.

"Investing money is not about getting rich quick," Ivy tells the twins in a wise voice. "It is about growing your money and having patience."

"There is one more thing I want to show you guys before we are done," Ivy says. She takes Milo and Mia by the hand and leads them to the biggest tree in the garden. She stops in front of it and looks up at it. Around the base of the tree are many different plants: some plants are small and have just started growing, while others are bigger and start looking like trees.

"This is what compound interest looks like," Ivy explains to the twins as they stand under the tree.

"Sometimes, when you invest, you earn compound interest," Ivy points to a fruit on the tree as it falls to the ground.

"The interest then grows into a new plant that can earn its own interest." Ivy shows the fruit on some of the plants under the big tree.

"Everything you see here is from one money seed being planted. This can only happen when we reinvest the money we make from the interest or profit on an investment." The twins turn in a circle, looking at all the plants around the big tree, amazed at everything coming from one seed.

Ivy walks the twins back to the start of the garden, where they first met her. "Thank you for visiting the Garden of Growth. It was an honor to teach you guys about investments." Ivy hugs each twin and turns to Goldie and Chip.

"You guys are doing wonderful work with them. You are welcome to the garden any time." Ivy gives one last round of hugs before she is covered in pink dust, returning to her original size, and flies away.

Learning with Milo and Mia.

Answer the questions below to see if you can remember what Ivy taught us in this chapter. Choose one correct answer below.

What three risk levels of investing do you get?

A. There is easy, hard, and extra hard.

B. You get low, moderate, and high-risk investments.

C. There are small, medium, and huge investments.

What does the best investment profile look like?

A. Only high-risk investments.

B. Only low-risk investments.

C. A mix of low, moderate, and high-risk investments.

What is compound interest?

A. It is when you invest something for the first time.

B. When you take your money out of the investment.

C. Money you earn from interest keeps growing because it adds to your original money and earns more interest over time.

Ask yourself these questions and think about your answers.

1. How is investing like planting a garden?

2. Why is patience important when you are investing?

Chapter 9

Valley of Loans

"What are we learning about next?" Mia asks Goldie as Goldie prepares a portal for them.

"Well, we have already covered a lot of things when it comes to money," Chip starts answering on account of Goldie concentrating on the portal.

"Now that you guys know how to save and invest money, you need to learn about borrowing money." Just then, Goldie finishes with her portal and calls everyone over.

"The portal is ready; let's move on to the next part of our adventure." Everyone steps through the portal, and with a pop, the portal closes behind them. They step out of the portal and arrive in a peaceful valley with rolling hills and sparkling streams.

There are cozy cottages scattered all over the landscape, each with its own little garden. Some of the cottages are connected to a bridge over the rivers. Suddenly, a big shadow falls over the valley.

The twins look up, trying to see what is causing the shadow. A big red dragon lands next to them, shaking the ground so much that Mia almost loses her balance. The dragon looms over them with a scary expression on his face, smoke coming out of his nostrils.

There is a flash of red and black, and the dragon is covered in smoke. Milo and Mia take a cautious step back, unsure what to expect next.

Out of the smoke steps a smaller, less intimidating dragon with a wide smile. He stretches out his hand and greets Goldie and Chip.

"Good friends, how wonderful to see you." He turns his attention to the twins, and his smile gets brighter.

"Hello, travelers," the red dragon waves at them. "I am Draco, and I watch over the Valley of Loans." He bows at them slightly.

"You're so cool," Milo whispers after he gets over the shock of seeing a dragon for the first time.

"Thank you," Draco laughs as he flexes his wings to make them look bigger. Milo is fascinated by this and steps closer to touch Draco's wings. Mia stops him before he can, reminding him that it is rude to touch someone without permission.

Milo looks at Draco with big eyes and asks if he can touch his wings. Draco nods his head yes, and Milo wastes no time.

"What do you do here in the valley, Draco?" Mia asks the dragon while her brother plays with his wings.

"I help people when they want to borrow money from the bank," Draco answers Mia. This gets the attention of Milo.

"Wait," Milo steps back from Draco's wings. "I didn't know you could borrow money from the bank." His eyes sparkle as he already thinks about all the things he can do with the money he borrows from the bank.

Draco laughs at the familiar look in Milo's eyes; it is a look he sees every time he helps people with their loans.

"Yes, you can borrow money from the bank." Milo starts moving from one leg to the other, excited to borrow money from the bank. Draco sees this and lifts his finger.

"Before you get excited and start planning what you are going to do with the money you borrow from the bank, there are a few things you need to know." Draco burst Milo's bubble. Mia put a reassuring hand on her brother's shoulder.

"Don't worry, Milo. Remember what we learned so far?" Mia tells her brother. "The more information we have, the better financial decisions we can make."

"That's right, Mia." Draco put a proud hand on Mia's head. "Borrowing money from the bank is a very serious thing, and we need to make sure that we do it right," Draco says sternly, wanting to make sure that the twins understand how important it is to make informed decisions when borrowing money.

"When we borrow money from the bank or from someone else, we are making a debt." Draco starts walking. "Borrowing money is like borrowing a tool from your neighbor. It helps you when you need it, but you need to give it back." Draco comes to a stop next to a bridge that leads to a beautiful cottage.

"There are two types of debt," Draco continues. "Do you want to take a guess what these types are, Milo?" Draco turns his attention to Milo, waiting for his answer.

Milo takes his time to think about Draco's question. He tries to remember if he has ever heard about debt before.

"You get big debt and small debt," Milo confidently answers Draco's question.

"That is a very good answer," Draco gives Milo a high-five.

"We do get big debt and small debt, but we also get good debt and bad debt," Draco tells the twins.

"Good debt is when you borrow money from the bank to do important things like buying a house," Draco points to the cottage on the other side of the bridge.

"You can also borrow money from the bank to pay for your education or even to open a business," Draco informs the twins.

"It is important to always do your research before you decide to borrow money," Draco cautions the twins. "For example, when you borrow money for your education, make sure that you will be able to get a good job with your degree, so you are able to pay your debt off."

He takes each twin by the hand and leads them over the bridge. On the other side of the bridge, and walks them over to the window of the cottage.

"Mia, can you tell me what bad debt might be?" Mia looks up at Draco as she ponders his question. She is not sure what bad debt is, but she thinks it has something to do with spending money irresponsibly.

"Is it when you buy things that you don't need?" Mia answers Draco. The dragon bends down and gives Mia a high-five.

"You're right, Mia. Bad debt is when we borrow money from the bank to make reckless or impulsive purchases."

"So, when I borrow money to go study to become a doctor, then we are making good debt. When we borrow money to buy a new gaming console, we are making bad debt." Chip speaks up, just as interested in learning and borrowing money as Milo and Mia.

"Yes, Chip. Now you are getting it." Draco opens the door to the cottage and walks in, inviting everyone to join him at the kitchen table. He pulls the tablet closer, which has been lying in the middle of the table.

"As nice as it is to have the option to borrow money from the bank, we still need to pay the money back."

Draco unlocks the tablet and puts it down so everyone can see the screen.

"When we borrow money, the bank will set up a payment plan so we can pay the money back." Mia leans closer to see the tablet better. She wants to open her own pet shop someday', so she needs to understand how this works in case she needs to borrow money.

"Often, you pay the money back over a few years." Draco continues.

"Some banks put interest in the money you need to pay back. Unlike with savings, interest on the money you borrow makes the amount you need to pay back bigger." Drago shows the twins an animated picture of a pile of money growing.

"The interest you pay goes to the bank for helping you and not back to you. Let's say you borrowed three gold coins from the bank. They can ask you to pay back four gold coins. The fourth coin is interest that the bank takes." Draco looks at everyone to make sure they understand him before he continues.

He taps on the screen a few times, and an official-looking document pops up.

"This is a loan agreement. Whenever you borrow money, you will get one of these. It is very important to read it first and make sure you understand everything before you borrow the money." Draco shows the screen to the twins and gives them time to get familiar with it.

"Before we even consider making a loan with the bank, we need to make sure that we can afford to pay them back," Draco warns the twins.

"Here, it shows you how much was borrowed from the bank," Draco points to a number on the page.

"And this is how much this person needs to pay back with the interest already included." The twin's eyes widen as they compare the two numbers.

"That is a lot of money," Mia whispers, shocked that someone can borrow so much money.

"It is, Mia. This person needs to pay back this money in seven years, and this is how much he will be paying every month." Draco shows the twins the rest of the document and sees the question in their eyes.

"Most of the time, you make a monthly payment to the bank for your loans, but you do have the option to pay it off more quickly if you want to." Draco finishes showing them the loan agreement. They all get up from the kitchen table, and Draco leads them outside. In a flash of red and black, Draco transforms back into the big dragon he is.

"Get on my back," he calls out in a booming voice to the twins, along with Chip and Goldie. They all get on his back, and as soon as the last person settles, they are off, flying through the sky.

The flight was over far too soon for Milo, who enjoyed being up in the sky. They land outside a cute bakery, and Draco turns into his smaller self.

He walks into the bakery, and the little bell above the door rings.

"Hello, Ellie," Draco calls out to a friendly lady packing cookies into the display case. The lady looks up and stops packing long enough to wave at them.

"Hello, Draco. I'll be right with you." She says as she disappears into the back. Milo and Mia explore the bakery as they wait for Ellie to return. Everything looks really yummy, and the air smells like freshly baked cookies and bread.

Ellie returns from the back with a tray filled with different cookies and some hot tea. She puts the tray down on a table and calls everyone over.

"Ellie, this is Milo and Mia. They are my interns for the day," Draco introduces the twins as they sit down to have some tea.

"Hello, Milo and Mia," Ellie greets the twins.

"Let's jump right into it, Ellie." Draco puts his tablet on the table and opens another official-looking document, this one similar to the one the twins saw earlier.

"You are doing really well with paying off your loan, Ellie," Draco compliments the bakery owner.

"This is how you will pay back the rest of your loan." The twins watch with rapid attention as Draco helps Ellie set up a new repayment plan for her loan. With this new plan, she can pay off her loan faster and still be able to put some money away to save.

"Do you want a tour of the bakery?" Ellie asks the twins after she and Draco finish discussing her new repayment plan. Milo and Mia nodded their heads excitedly.

Mia wonders if Ellie's bakery looks the same as the one they worked in while they were in the District of Jobs with Jaxon.

As they walk around the bakery, Ellie starts pointing to the things she bought using the money she borrowed from the bank. Mia was impressed by everything she saw. The more time she spent with Ellie, the better Mia understood why someone would want to take out a loan for their business.

They finally move to the back, where everything is being made.

"This oven here is the entire reason I took out a loan with the bank," Ellie tells the twins.

"My bakery was doing so well that I couldn't bake enough treats to satisfy all my customers because my oven was too small." Ellie points to an oven that looks a lot like the one the twins have in their kitchen back home.

"Luckily for me, Draco is an excellent financial advisor and helped me with taking out a loan from the bank. If it wasn't for Draco's help, I would never have been able to grow my business as much as I did," Ellie gives Draco a thankful hug.

Ellie gives them all a small box of cookies and waves goodbye as they walk out of the bakery. Draco leads the way as they walk to a park nearby to enjoy their delicious cookies.

"What happens when you don't pay the bank on time?" Milo asks as they walk.

"Well, when we borrow money and pay the money back on time, we build up trust with the banks," Draco explains, taking a seat in the shade under a big tree in the park.

"This trust makes it easier to borrow money again in the future. If we don't pay back the money we borrowed, we lose this trust in the banks, which makes it difficult for us to borrow money again," Draco finishes his explanation.

The twins enjoy their cookies with Goldie, Chip, and Draco.

Before, they had a little pop quiz. Draco reminds them that they should only borrow money for things that are truly important and only when they are sure they can pay it back.

After their pop quiz, they say goodbye to Draco. Milo and Mia are excited to find out what their next adventure will be.

Learning with Milo and Mia.

Answer the questions below to see if you can remember what Draco taught us in this chapter. Choose one correct answer below.

What types of debt do we get?

A. There is good debt and bad debt.

B. There is only one type of debt, the expensive type.

C. We should not be making debt.

What is an example of good debt?

A. When you take out a loan to buy a house.

B. Borrowing money to buy a gaming console.

C. Borrowing money to go see your favorite music star.

Should we pay the money back we borrowed from the bank?

A. No, the money is yours now.

B. Yes, it is important to pay the money back on time.

C. Yes, but you can pay the money back whenever you want to.

Ask yourself these questions and think about your answers.

1. How can borrowing money help you?

2. What is important to remember when you borrow money?

Chapter 10

Field of Trust

Milo and Mia no longer ask their guides about what they will learn next. Instead, they close their eyes as they jump through the portal that Goldie made for them.

Once on the other side, the twins take in everything with wide eyes. No matter how many places they visit, they always seem amazed when they go to the next one. Milo and Mia find themselves standing in a big field that stretches further than the eye can see.

The place is filled with beautiful gardens, neat pathways, and buildings that sparkle in the sun. All around them are trees with different-colored leaves on their branches. The twins are still busy admiring the scenery when they hear someone calling out to them.

"Hello, friends." Milo and Mia turn around to see who is calling out to them. They come face-to-face with a fairy. This fairy looks a little different from Ivy, the fairy they met in the Garden of Growth.

"My name is Claire, and I run the credit department here in the Valley of Trust." Claire sticks out her hand for a handshake with the twins. Milo looks over at Goldie, who gives him an encouraging nod; he extends his hand and shakes Claire's. She smiles brightly at him and turns her attention to Mia.

"Who might you be?" Claire asks as she shakes Mia's hand. Mia clears her throat and points to herself.

"My name is Mia, and that is my twin brother, Milo." After shaking the fairy's hand, Mia notices her wings for the first time. She gasped and took a shocked step back.

"Are your wings gold?" Mia asks Claire; she has never seen wings like those before. Claire shakes her head and gives Mia a knowing smile.

"Yes, they are gold." Claire spins in a slow circle to give Mia a better look at the wings.

"Here in the Valley of Trust, we use these gold leaves to buy things." Claire opens the small pouch on her hip and takes two gold leaves out of it.

"We call these trust leaves. My wings are made of them." Claire flutters her wings to emphasize her point.

"That is why they made me the head fairy of the credit department," Claire tells the twins.

Goldie clears her throat and catches Claire's attention. With a smile and a bounce in her step, Claire walks over to Goldie and Chip.

"Hello, Goldie." Claire gives a hug to Goldie.

"Hello, Chip." The tips of Claire's ears turn a light pink as she gives Chip his hug.

"Hello, Claire. It's nice to see you again." Chip smiles at Claire after she lets go of the hug. The credit fairy stares at Chip for a while before she shakes herself out of it.

"Anyway," Claire fiddles with her dress, keeping her eyes down. When she is happy that her dress is straight and neat, Claire looks back up at the twins with a smile.

"Can you tell me what it means to buy something on credit?" Claire looks at the twins expectantly, waiting for one of them to answer her question.

"I think it means you buy something now but promise to pay for it later," Milo answers Claire's question.

He remembers Draco talking about needing good credit to get a loan to buy things like a house.

"That's right, Milo," Claire gives Milo a fist bump.

"When you buy something on credit, you get the thing now and pay for it later." Claire takes the twins by the hand and starts walking toward the trees with different colored leaves.

"We should be mindful of the things we buy using credit." They reach the trees with colorful leaves and come to a stop.

"The gold trust leaves we use here in the Valley of Trust are like using a credit card." Claire points to the trees in front of the twins, which have different leaves. "Every color on these trees represents a credit limit." Milo puts his hand in the air, wanting to ask Claire a question.

"Yes, Milo?"

"What is a credit limit?" Milo asks Claire, his eyes not leaving the colorful trees in front of him.

"A credit limit is how much money you can borrow on your credit card before you need to pay it back." Claire reaches up and takes two different colored leaves from the tree. She shows the first leave to the twins; this leaf is a light blue color.

"When you get this leaf, it means your credit limit is two gold coins." She hands the light blue leaf over to Milo to look at it closely.

"This means that you can buy something that costs two gold coins. If the thing you want costs more than two gold coins, you will have to look for something else to buy." Claire hands the second leaf over to Mia; this one is a dark purple color.

"That leaf has a credit limit of four gold coins. Remember, everyone's credit limit is different." After the twins are done looking at the credit limit leaves, Claire takes it and puts it back on the tree.

Claire gets down on her knees and looks the twins in the eyes.

"Having a trust leaf and buying on credit is a big responsibility," Claire cautions the twins. Milo and Mia nod their heads, understanding the weight of having a trust leave. Satisfied with the twins' reaction, Claire reaches into her pouch filled with trust leaves. She takes out two and gives each twin a leaf.

"Buying stuff you need on credit can be very useful," Claire tells the twins as they admire their gold trust leaves.

"This trust leaf represents a promise you make to the bank to pay back the money you borrow when you buy something." Claire looks from one twin to the other, making sure they are listening to her.

"Just like when you take out a loan with a bank, you need to pay back the money you borrow on time." Milo and Mia nod their heads at Claire; they start to understand the reason for having a trust leave a bit better.

Claire leads the twins, along with Goldie and Chip, to a market just over the hill. By now, Milo and Mia have an idea of what to expect. They look up at Claire and wait for her to explain what they will be doing next.

Claire reaches into her pouch and takes out a light blue leaf from the Tree of Credit Limits. She hands one to Milo and one to Mia.

"For today, your credit limit is two gold coins each. A credit limit tells you how much you can buy on credit; you don't have to use it all in one go." Milo and Mia nod at Claire as they take the credit limit leaves.

"You can buy anything from these stalls as long as your purchase does not exceed your credit limit," Claire tells them with a firm look.

The twins thank Claire and walk to the first stall to see what they are selling. Milo and Mia take their time as they go through the stalls, looking for something to buy.

Milo stopped at a stall selling awesome bicycles and saw one he really wanted while they were walking around the market. Milo points to the bicycle he wants and asks the stall attendant if he can get the bicycle on credit.

"I am sorry, boy. You don't have enough trust leaves. You need to increase your credit score. That way, you have a higher limit you can use to buy things on credit," the vendor says remorsefully to Milo. Milo turns away, disappointed; he really wanted that bicycle. Claire sees his disappointment and calls him and Mia over to ask Milo what happened.

"I wanted to buy a bicycle, but the vendor said my credit score was not high enough," Milo says with a pout.

"I don't even know what a credit score is," Milo tells Claire. The fairy gives Milo a soft smile and bends down to be at eye level with him.

"A credit score is a number that shows people how much they can trust you to pay back the money you borrow." Claire stands upright as she continues explaining credit scores to the twins.

"If you have a high score, people know they can trust you to pay the money back. If your score is low, they might choose not to lend you money because they don't know if you will pay the money back."

"How do you get a good credit score?" Mia puts her hand in the air, asking Claire a question.

"You can earn a good credit score by paying the money back on time and not borrowing more money than you can pay," Claire explains.

"As soon as you borrow more money than you can pay or you forget to pay the money back, then your credit score drops. If you are not careful, people may refuse to lend you money."

The twins nod their heads at Claire's explanation. Milo feels better knowing why the vendor did not want to sell him the bicycle.

"Let's play a game." Claire reaches into her pouch and takes out some more gold leaves. She hands a few to Milo and some to Mia.

"The aim of the game is to get your credit score as high as you can by buying things on credit and paying them off as soon as you can." Claire reaches into her pouch again and takes out two watches.

"You will be able to track your credit score on these watches." She helps the twins put on the watches and shows them how they work. Once they are ready, Claire starts a countdown.

"Three, two, one. Go!" Milo and Mia jump away and run to the market. Each twin goes their own way to try to find the best deals and build up their credit at the same time.

Mia heads over to a series of stalls filled with dolls and dresses. She wants to find a dress for herself that matches a doll. Milo, on the other hand, heads over to an adventure stall and decides to use his credit for an experience, so he goes go-karting.

Both twins enjoy building up their credit scores by paying back what they bought on credit. They make sure to keep track of their spending so that they don't go over what they are able to pay back.

The twins come back together and compare everything they bought on credit to see who has the best credit score.

"Look, Milo! I got us some new board games, a new doll, and this beautiful dress." Mia shows her brother and Claire all the beautiful things she has bought on credit. "The dress even matches the dress of my new doll!"

Claire compliments Mia's new dress and takes a look at her credit score.

"You did very well, Mia. You used your credit wisely and paid everything off on time."

"My turn!" Milo jumps up and down, excited to show everyone what he got by using his credit.

"I went go-karting and got this awesome picture." Milo shows a picture of him sitting in a red go-kart to the group.

"I also got this cool new dinosaur and these new shoes!" Milo shows them his new shoes, which light up with a bright smile.

"I went back to the vendor who was selling the bicycle. He said my credit score was high enough so I could get the one I wanted!" Milo steps to the side and shows everyone.

"That is amazing, Milo," Claire praises Milo. "This shows you that you can build up your credit to get the things you want. Come, let me look at your credit score so we can choose a winner." Claire takes Milo's watch and compares it to Mia's.

"Congratulations, Milo. You are the winner of our little game." Milo cheers and hugs Claire, happy that he won the game. Chip gives him a fist bump, and Goldie hugs him.

"Thank you for coming to the Valley of Trust. Remember, credit takes longer to build up back in the real world, so you need to be patient. I really enjoyed teaching you guys about buying things on credit." Mia walks over and gives Claire a hug, thanking her for being such a good teacher.

After Claire waves goodbye to everyone, Goldie opens the portal so they can move on to their next adventure.

"The next part of our journey is always my favorite," Goldie tells the twins as they walk through the portal.

"We will be learning about planning for the future and setting financial goals."

Learning with Milo and Mia.

Answer the questions below to see if you can remember what Claire taught us in this chapter. Choose one correct answer below.

What does it mean to buy something on credit?

A. Credit is when your mom gives you pocket money.
B. When you save money to buy something later.
C. It is when you borrow money to buy something you need and pay it back later.

How do you build good credit?

A. When you borrow more money than you can pay back.

B. By paying the money off on time and not borrowing more than you can pay back.

C. By not paying the money back.

What is a credit score?

A. It is a number that shows how much money we have.

B. it is the name of your math marks in school.

C. It is a score that shows how good you are at paying back the money you borrow.

Ask yourself these questions and think about your answers.

1. What can happen if you don't pay back your credit on time?

2. What are some examples of things we can buy on credit?

Chapter 11

Hall of Dreams

Milo and Mia step out of the portal and into a grand hall with the tallest walls Milo has ever seen. Scattered around the hall are floating orbs of light. The orbs are different colors, and some of them glow brighter than others.

"Where are we, Goldie?" Mia asks as she steps closer to a floating orb, curious to see what it is. She tries to touch the orb, but it slowly moves away from her.

"You are in the Hall of Dreams," an unfamiliar voice behind Mia answers the question. Mia spins around to find a middle-aged woman smiling down at her. Her face turns red; Mia is a little embarrassed for being caught trying to touch the orbs.

"Hello, dear. My name is Gloria. Who might you be?" Gloria wears big round glasses on her face, and her blond hair is in a beautiful braid down her back. Mia does a double take; Gloria looks just like her favorite art teacher, Miss Abigail.

"I'm Mia." Gloria greets her with a serene head nod. Mia gives a little wave and smiles back at Gloria. Milo walks over to where the two are standing and squints at Gloria.

"You look a lot like our art teacher, Miss Abigail." Milo voices what Mia has been thinking as he walks around Gloria to see her from all sides.

Gloria raises her eyebrow at Milo, not saying anything as she waits for him to introduce himself. When Gloria pulls her face like that, she is an exact copy of Miss Abigail. Milo cannot figure out why she is looking at him like that until Mia pokes him in his side.

He looks over at his sister, who is pulling her face at him.

"Introduce yourself," Mia whispers under her breath.

"Oh yeah, my name is Milo." Gloria laughs at Milo as he introduces himself, delighted by his carefree nature.

Goldie catches Gloria's attention. "Will you please look after these two while we quickly head out to prepare something?" Goldie points to herself and Chip. Gloria nods her head, and then Goldie opens a portal, promising the twins that they will be back soon.

"What do you do here, anyway?" Milo asks Gloria.

Gloria is starting to get the impression that Milo loves asking questions, while Mia is more of a listening type. It is a good thing that she loves answering questions.

"I love helping people reach their dreams," Gloria answers Milo as she looks around the room. "I do that by teaching people how to set up financial goals and stick to them."

Milo wrinkles his nose at Gloria's answer, "Why do you need to set goals when you are saving money? Can't you just save it?" Milo looks over at his sister to see if she shares the same thinking.

Mia shrugs her shoulders and gives her attention to Gloria, also wondering why you need a plan to save.

"When you set a savings goal for yourself, it motivates you to save more and not spend the money you have already saved." Gloria looks at all the floating orbs around her one more time.

She is very proud of the work she does. It brings her a lot of happiness when people light up as they write out their saving goals and plans.

"Every orb you see today represents someone's savings goals. The brighter an orb shines, the closer the person is to reaching the goal they have been saving for." Gloria points to the orbs around them.

Milo and Mia marvel at the orbs. They have never seen anything like this before. Mia is still wondering what is keeping the orbs floating. Are they using strings?

One orb is shining brighter than the rest, catching Mia's attention. She steps closer to it and tries to touch it lightly with her finger. This time, the orb does not float away. The orb is not what she expected at all. It is slightly warm to the touch and bobs up and down when she touches it.

"Gloria, why is this orb so bright? Are they almost done saving?" Mia asks Gloria over her shoulder, her attention still captured by the orb. Gloria comes to stand behind Mia and looks at the orb.

She claps her hands in excitement.

"This person is very close to reaching their savings goal. They only need to save one more time, and then their goal will be completed." Gloria smiles down at Mia.

"What happens when they are done saving?" Milo asks as he starts poking the orb Mia is looking at. Gloria lightly catches his hand to stop him from continuing.

"As soon as they are done saving, the orb will shoot into the sky and become a star, ready for them to wish upon and have their dreams come true." Mia looks up at the roof of the hall and realizes for the first time that there is no roof. The night sky expands far above their heads, twinkling with too many stars to count.

"Wow," Mia breathes out. She has always loved the stars. Seeing them like this gives her a new appreciation for them. It warms her heart to think that so many people have already saved enough money to reach their dreams.

"Come on, there is something I would like to show you." Gloria leads the group around the border of the hall. The walls of the hall are filled with different types of doors and arches leading to different rooms. Gloria walks to the first door and opens it, waving everyone into the room.

"There are different goals we can set to save money. This is the room for short-term goals." The room is filled with floating orbs, much like the ones in the hall. The orbs in the room are small in comparison to the orbs in the hall.

"Why are all these orbs small?" Milo asks the question before Mia can, much to Gloria's amusement.

"They are small because the money the person needs to save is small," Gloria explains to the twins.

"When you set a short-term saving goal for yourself, it is usually for small things like buying a tasty treat or small toys. It is money you put away that you want to use in the next few weeks." The room lights up as one orb after the other starts shooting into the sky. Milo and Mia gasp at the big number of orbs shooting into the sky.

"It is easy to reach short-term saving goals, and by completing a few, you can motivate yourself to save more money for your medium and long-term goals," Gloria tells the twins as she leads them out of the room and toward the next one.

They walk into the next room. This room looks the same as the previous one, with orbs floating around.

Milo walks up to one orb and inspects it closely, trying to see if he can guess what the person is saving for.

The orbs in this room are bigger than those in the short-term savings room but still not as big as the orbs outside in the hall.

"As you can see, the orbs in this room are bigger. This means that these goals need a bit more money before they are completed," Gloria points out.

"All the orbs in here represent a medium-term goal. These saving goals usually take a bit longer to save for, like buying a new bike or saving for a new gaming console." Gloria gives the twins time to take everything in before she moves on. They walk out of the room and come to a stop in the big hall again.

"You have already seen the orbs in here." Milo and Mia look at the hall with new eyes, now understanding what is happening better.

"In here are all the long-term goals," Gloria tells the twins.

"The long-term saving goals are for very important and big things, like saving for your education or buying a home," Gloria explains to Milo and Mia.

"It is very hard to save for these things if you don't have a plan set out to help you stay on track." Gloria pulls two pieces of paper out of thin air, winking at the shocked expressions on Milo and Mia's faces.

"I will show you how to set up your own financial goals and help you plan how you will be saving." Milo and Mia take the papers from Gloria and move to take seats at two desks that appear out of thin air, just like the papers.

"This is a goal chart. Think of your goal chart as a treasure map that shows each step to reach your savings goal. You write your goals down here," Gloria points to the top of the page. "And you write your saving plan here."

"What do you guys want to save for?" Milo and Mia take their time to think about what they want to save money for.

"I want to save money for a new bike," Milo is the first one to answer. Mia is still thinking about what she wants to save for.

Gloria helps Milo write down his savings goal and set up a savings plan to reach the goal. Milo decides that he will save money to buy himself a new gaming console.

Gloria shows him how the goal tracker works and how much money he needs to save every month.

"I think I want to save to buy my mom something pretty for her birthday," Mia finally decides what she wants to save money for. Gloria smiles at her and helps her set up a goal and savings plan.

By the end of the exercise, Milo and Mia have personalized saving goals and are excited to start saving.

"Thank you so much for showing us how to set goals. It was really fun," Mia thanked Gloria and hugged her tightly. Goldie is opening the portal to their next destination in the background.

"It's my pleasure; it was nice having you guys here. I can't wait to see your savings grow brighter as you get closer to your goals." Gloria waves goodbye to the twins, and they disappear through the portal.

Learning with Milo and Mia.

Answer the questions below to see if you can remember what Gloria taught us in this chapter. Choose one correct answer below.

Why is it important to have goals?

A. So you can draw pretty pictures.

B. Goals help to motivate you to save and keep you on track.

C. It helps you with your math homework.

What type of goals do you get?

A. Goals that are tasty to eat.

B. You get pink goals, blue goals, and orange goals.

C. You get short, medium, and long-term goals.

What is an example of a long-term goal?

A. Saving money to buy yourself a treat.

B. Saving money to buy a home.

C. Saving money for a bike.

Ask yourself these questions and think about your answers.

1. What is one financial goal you have?

2. How can you start saving for this financial goal?

Chapter 12

Land of Giving

Milo and Mia find themselves standing in what looks like a school courtyard. The air is filled with laughter and music; kids of all ages are running around and playing. The courtyard is covered with colorful banners and a lot of tables.

Some people are busy setting tables, helping people sign documents, and taking what looks like boxes of supplies. Other people play games with the kids and talk to each other as they walk around.

At closer inspection, the twins notice that the tables are all different. There are tables where you can drop off food for cats and dogs and other tables are collecting non-perishable foods and clothes.

A Koala walks up to the group with a clipboard in her hand. She smiles at Goldie and Chip, shaking their hands before turning to the twins.

"Hello, you must be Milo and Mia." The koala sticks out her hand to shake theirs. "I am Kindness; it is nice to meet you." Kindness looks down at her clipboard.

"I see you guys are here for a tour." She smiles at the twins and hands them each a flyer that she takes from her clipboard.

"Welcome to the Land of Giving, where giving back to the community is the wind in our sails." With a flourish, Kindness turns around and showcases the different stalls.

"Giving back to the community is something we choose to do; no one can force us to give, and we should not try to force others to give," Kindness tells the twins in a serious voice.

"By giving back, we help the world become a better place for ourselves and others." Kindness leads them to a table collecting canned goods.

"There are many different ways we can give back. One of these ways is by donating things." Kindness points to the table they are standing next to.

"You can donate non-perishable foods, clothing, and even toys you are no longer using." They watch as a family of four gives boxes filled with food to the person attending the table.

"Remember, when you are donating things like clothing and toys, make sure they are clean and safe for others to use." Kindness ticks something off on her clipboard and starts walking. The twins follow her, seeing more tables like the one they just visited.

"Can you donate other things?" Milo asks Kindness curiously.

"Yes, Milo. You can donate almost anything. If it is something you no longer need or use, you can donate it instead of throwing it away," Kindness answers Milo with a smile.

They move on to the next table, where people write their names on a list and walk away.

"Why are they writing their names down?" Mia asks as she tries to get a better view of the table.

"They are putting their names on a list to do volunteer work," Kindness explains. They wait for the person in front of them to finish before they step up.

"Hello, Kindness. It's lovely to see you." The stall owner greets Kindness.

"Good afternoon, Shane. Please tell these two young ones what your volunteer program is about," Shane's eyes brighten at Kindness's request. He nods and hands a flyer over to Milo and Mia.

"We help people find the perfect volunteering fit," Shane points down to the flyer in their hands.

"When you sign up with us, you tell us about the things you are passionate about, and we help you find the perfect non-profit organization where you can volunteer," Shane continues to tell them about his stall.

"What is volunteering?" Milo asks.

"Volunteering is when you work at a non-profit organization, but you don't get paid for it," Chip says, answering for Shane.

"For example, when you go to this animal non-profit organization, you will help them with things like feeding the animals and cleaning their cages," Shane points to a section on his flyer with information about an animal rescue non-profit.

"A non-profit organization?" Mia asks Kindness, a little confused. The twins are learning a lot of new words today.

"A non-profit organization is a group that doesn't keep any extra money as profit. Instead, it uses any money it makes to support its activities or mission. Some non-profits help people or protect nature, while others bring people together for hobbies or activities they enjoy," Kindness explains, but the twins still look a little confused.

"Non-profit organizations, for example, open up a soup shop to feed homeless people and use the money they make to keep the soup shop open." Kindness clarifies for the twins.

With the help of Shane and Kindness, the twins each sign up to volunteer at one non-profit organization. Mia decides to volunteer at the animal shelter, and Milo signs his name up to help out at their local fire station.

They thanked Shane for his help and moved on to the next stall. This stall is a lot like Shane's. You also sign your name up to help people, but with this one, it is all about the skills you have.

"When we offer our skills to people, we help them in a very specific way. A very good example of this is Doctors Without Borders." The stall attendant explains to the twins.

When they are done looking at all the stalls and donating some things, Kindness leads them to a big tent in the middle of the courtyard.

"We are busy planning a fundraiser for a children's hospital. Will you please help us organize it?" Kindness asks Milo and Mia as they enter the tent. The twins agree with smiles, eager to help Kindness.

With the help of Chip and Goldie, the twins decide to have a fun fair to raise the money they need for the children's hospital.

The fun fair will be filled with food, games, and even entertainment. After making all the arrangements, Milo and Mia help the vendors set up their stalls and start handing out flyers to inform people about the upcoming fun fair.

Dedicated booths for donations are set up around the courtyard to encourage people to give.

As everything comes together, Milo and Mia decide to use their skills to help the cause. They speak to the person in charge of the entertainment and arrange that they do a magic show for the crowd.

Milo and Mia spend the next twenty minutes entertaining the crow with their magic tricks, making it laugh whenever Milo tells a joke. The twins have never had as much fun as they are having now.

"That was amazing! I didn't know you could do magic, Mia," Goldie compliments the twins on their craftsmanship as they step off the stage. Mia beams at the compliment and does a little bow for Chip.

Kindness walks over to the twins with a tablet in her hand.

"Well done, guys! We have exceeded the donation goal we have set up for the day." Kindness shows them the tablet with the donation amount on it. Milo and Mia's eyes grow wide when they see how much money they have helped raise for the children's hospital. It is way more than they needed.

"What will happen with all the money?" Milo asks Kindness, still amazed at all the money they raised.

"We will be using this money to buy new medical supplies for the hospital and some toys and games for the children to make their stay more comfortable," Kindness explains to the twins.

"If there is any money left, it will be used for other things the children's hospital might need." Milo and Mia are happy with Kindness's answer and hug her.

"Thank you for showing us how important it is to give back to the community." Mia looks up at Kindness as she hugs her. "You are awesome." She whispers her compliment to Kindness under her breath.

Kindness says goodbye to the twins and disappears into the crowd, already planning her next fundraiser.

"That was so fun! Where are we going next?" Milo asks Goldie as she opens a final portal.

"We are going home," Goldie tells the twins. Milo and Mia nod their heads and step through the portal.

They are a little sad that their adventure is ending, but they can't wait to tell their parents and grandparents about everything.

Learning with Milo and Mia.

Answer the questions below to see if you can remember what Kindness taught us in this chapter. Choose one correct answer below.

What does volunteering mean?

A. It is dancing in the school play.

B. It is when you clean the kitchen for your mom.

C. It is when you do work for an organization without getting paid.

Why is it important to give back to the community?

A. It helps us make money.

B. By giving back to the community, we are making the world a better place.

C. Because our parents tell us to.

What are some examples of donations?

A. Helping the dog shelter by cleaning the cages.

B. You can donate money, toys, or even non-perishable food.

C. Washing someone's car for them.

Ask yourself these questions and think about your answers.

1. How does sharing make you feel?
2. What are some ways you can help others by sharing?

Epilogue

Milo and Mia step out of the portal for the final time. They are back in their grandparents' attic and can hear their family moving around downstairs.

"This is where we say goodbye," Goldie tells the twins with a sad smile on her face. She really enjoyed spending time with the twins and Chip as they went on their adventures. Milo and Mia say goodbye to Goldie and Chip, promising them that they will come and play in the attic again. In a flash of light, Goldie and Chip disappear, and the twins make their way to the kitchen.

Milo and Mia talk about their adventure all the way to the kitchen. They are excited about everything they learned and feel a sense of accomplishment for completing everything. They can't wait to share their adventures with their parents.

"Milo, Mia, welcome back!" Their mother greets them as they enter the kitchen.

"Hold up, you two. One at a time, please." The mother laughs at them. She leads them to the kitchen table and sits down. Milo's and Mia's father joins them at the table, and their grandparents stay standing at the kitchen counter.

"We went on the coolest adventure ever, Mom!" Milo is the first to speak up. He tells them all about the magical land they visited.

"Goldie and Chip took us through this portal thing, and then we got to meet a King who taught us all about money and where it comes from!" Milo speaks very fast and barely breathes.

"And then we met this Queen lady that gave us cool piggy banks; mine glows in the dark," Milo continues his recall of their adventure without giving anyone a chance to speak.

"Mom helped us open a savings account, and we learned how to search for good deals and save money." Milo is reenacting their search for deals, and the twins' parents and grandparents laugh at his silliness.

"My favorite part was working on the construction site and getting paid!" Milo finally finishes his story and takes a deep breath, his eyes shining brightly.

Mia jumps in where Milo left off, giving their parents no other choice but to listen to her story as well.

She tells them about the beautiful garden filled with people's investments and learning how to set saving goals. Mia tells them all about credit scores and how they work. She finishes her story by telling her parents about giving back to the community and asks if they can take her to the local charity shop so she can donate some of her toys and dresses that she no longer uses.

"Of course, honey. There is a charity shop very close to your school. We will make a stop there and ask them how their donations work," Mia's mom says as she tucks Mia's hair behind her ear.

"I am super proud of you two," Their dad reaches over, runs his hand through Milo's hair, and kisses Mia on her head. The twins smile up at their dad; they are happy that they were able to make their dad proud.

"It is important to remember that learning to work with money is a lifelong journey." their father reminds them in a gentle voice.

Their grandmother tells them that dinner is ready, and everyone sits around the table. The air is filled with

laughter and stories as the adults recall their own adventures with money.

After dinner, Milo, Mia, and their parents all walk home. As soon as they get home, the twins head up to their rooms to get ready for bed.

Long after their parents have gone to bed, Milo sneaks into his sister's room and lies down next to her.

"Do you think we will see Goldie and Chip again?" he whispers to his sister. He really enjoyed going on the magical adventure and wants to do another one again.

Mia lies on her bed and looks up at the glowing stars on the roof of her room, thinking about his question before she whispers back.

"Yeah, I think we will go on many adventures with them." Milo gives Mia a high-five, and they get into bed, wondering when their next adventure with Goldie and Chip will be.

Ask yourself these questions and think about your answers.

1. What was the most important lesson Milo and Mia learned during their adventures?

Multiple Choice Answers

Chapter 1
1. A
2. A
3. B

Chapter 2
1. B
2. A
3. B

Chapter 3
1. A
2. C
3. B

Chapter 4
1. B
2. A
3. C

Chapter 5
1. C
2. C
3. A

Chapter 6
1. A
2. C
3. B

Chapter 7
1. A
2. B
3. C

Chapter 8
1. B
2. C
3. C

Chapter 9
1. A
2. A
3. B

Chapter 10
1. C
2. B
3. C

Chapter 11
1. B
2. C
3. B

Chapter 12
1. C
2. B
3. B

Share the Adventure!

Thank you for joining Mia and Milo on their exciting financial adventure! We hope you enjoyed learning about budgeting, saving, investing, and all the fun lessons along the way.

If you found this story engaging and valuable, your honest review can help other parents and young readers discover this book and start their own journey to financial literacy. Your thoughts not only mean the world to us but also inspire future adventurers to learn, grow, and dream big.

We'd love to hear what you think—whether it's about your favorite character, the most surprising lesson, or how this story made an impact. Thank you for being part of Mia and Milo's financial literacy adventure!

Until next time, keep learning and growing!

References

Beattie, A. (2024, September 24). *The history of money: bartering to banknotes to bitcoin. Investopedia.* https://www.investopedia.com/articles/07/roots_of_money.asp

6-ways-to-save-money-as-a-Kid. (n.d.). https://www.gohenry.com/uk/blog/financial-education/6-ways-to-save-money-as-a-kid

A comprehensive guide to teaching kids about banking. (n.d.). Digit Insurance. https://www.godigit.com/life-insurance/child-insurance-plans/savings/teaching-kids-about-banking

Kids and money: Wants vs. needs. (2022, September 19). NDSU Agriculture. https://www.ndsu.edu/agriculture/extension/publications/kids-and-money-wants-vs-needs

Teaching kids to spend: Part 2 - store comparisons - National Bank of Mom. (n.d.). National Bank of Mom. https://nationalbankofmom.com/teach-kids-spend-store-comparison-price/

What-is-compound-interest. (n.d.). https://www.gohenry.com/us/blog/financial-education/what-is-compound-interest-explaining-to-kids-and-teens

Made in the USA
Coppell, TX
01 January 2025

43792450R00098